T0360726

Absolute Essentials of Business Ethics

This shortform textbook explores practical applications of how business ethics impacts working lives, allowing readers to reflect on their own moral compass through the use of ethical dilemmas.

Highlighting the extensive breadth of issues related to business ethics, the authors introduce and analyze ethical and unethical behaviors of firms through numerous real-life examples including Patagonia, Costco, LVMH, Bill Gates, Muhummad Yunus, Enron, WorldCom, Samsung, Purdue Pharma, Vale Mining, and the COVID-19 crisis.

Regardless of career path or occupation, *Absolute Essentials of Business Ethics* is a valuable resource to understand why people make decisions based on their own ethical values and beliefs. Useful at both undergraduate and graduate levels, this unique textbook will serve students of business ethics around the world.

Peter A. Stanwick is Associate Professor of Management at Auburn University, USA. He is co-author of *Understanding Business Ethics*, *International Management: A Stakeholder Perspective*, and *Corporate Sustainability Leadership*.

Sarah D. Stanwick is Associate Professor of Accounting at Auburn University, USA. She is co-author of *Understanding Business Ethics*, *International Management: A Stakeholder Perspective*, and *Corporate Sustainability Leadership*.

Absolute Essentials of Business and Economics

Textbooks are an extraordinarily useful tool for students and teachers, as is demonstrated by their continued use in the classroom and online. Successful textbooks run into multiple editions, and in endeavouring to keep up with developments in the field, it can be difficult to avoid increasing length and complexity.

This series of shortform textbooks offers a range of books which zero-in on the absolute essentials. In focusing on only the core elements of each sub-discipline, the books provide a useful alternative or supplement to traditional textbooks.

Titles in this series include:

Absolute Essentials of Digital Marketing
Alan Charlesworth

Absolute Essentials of International Business
Alan Sitkin & Karine Mangion

Absolute Essentials of Project Management
Paul Roberts

Absolute Essentials of Business Behavioural Ethics
Nina Seppala

Absolute Essentials of Corporate Governance
Stephen Bloomfield

Absolute Essentials of Business Ethics
Peter A. Stanwick & Sarah D. Stanwick

For more information about this series, please visit: www.routledge.com/Absolute-Essentials-of-Business-and-Economics/book-series/ABSOLUTE

Absolute Essentials of Business Ethics

Peter A. Stanwick and
Sarah D. Stanwick

Routledge
Taylor & Francis Group

LONDON AND NEW YORK

First published 2021
by Routledge
2 Park Square, Milton Park, Abingdon, Oxon OX14 4RN

and by Routledge
52 Vanderbilt Avenue, New York, NY 10017

Routledge is an imprint of the Taylor & Francis Group, an informa business

© 2021 Peter A. Stanwick and Sarah D. Stanwick

The right of Peter A. Stanwick and Sarah D. Stanwick to be identified as authors of this work has been asserted by them in accordance with sections 77 and 78 of the Copyright, Designs and Patents Act 1988.

British Library Cataloguing-in-Publication Data
A catalogue record for this book is available from the British Library

Library of Congress Cataloging-in-Publication Data
A catalog record has been requested for this book

ISBN: 978-0-367-41474-0 (hbk)
ISBN: 978-0-367-81466-3 (ebk)

Typeset in Bembo
by Newgen Publishing UK

To my parents, Casey and Olive, who taught me the value of hard work and getting a good education.

To the love of my life, Sarah, my soulmate and guiding light for over three decades.

To our children, Olivia and John, whose love and support are unconditional.

To our dachshund, Belle, who has provided us more joy than any family deserves.

Peter

This book is dedicated to the ones I love, but especially to Peter, Olivia, John, Belle, Kathy, and David; and in memory of Edna and Doc, the best parents a person could hope for.

Sarah

Contents

Introduction

Absolute Essentials of Business Ethics presents a practical application of how business ethics impacts people in their daily lives. Through theoretical concepts and real-life examples, this book captures the essence of the impact ethical beliefs have on society.

While shortform in nature, this book presents detailed relevant concepts in a condensed format. The practical nature of the writing style allows the reader to quickly understand the interaction between ethical values and the decision-making process of individuals.

The potential audiences for *Absolute Essentials of Business Ethics* are three-fold. The first is students in either undergraduate or graduate-level business classes. By focusing on the most relevant ethical topics, this book serves as an effective reference as either a primary or secondary source of material for business classes.

The second audience for this book is students interested in a supplement for non-business-related curriculums. The interaction of business and ethics impacts all undergraduate and graduate-level classes regardless of the subject area of the class.

The third audience is anyone interested in learning more about business ethics. Regardless of your career path or occupation, this book will inform you and enrich your ability to understand the complex relationships between business and ethics.

From its theoretical foundation in Chapter 1 through to the exploration of environmental sustainability and the developing world in later chapters, this book guides the reader through a journey which can incite emotions including joy, anger, disbelief, despair, happiness, amazement, and satisfaction. As with any journey, this book provides both emotional highs and lows as the reader comprehends both the local and global impact of business ethics.

Using this book

The foundational structure of *Absolute Essentials of Business Ethics* is based on the perspective of stakeholders. Stakeholders, who are any individuals with a vested interest in the operations of the firm, guide (or should guide) the decisions and actions of the firm.

Therefore, the book builds on the philosophical foundation of ethics with the initial extension to address the role of stakeholders and corporate social responsibility. The book then moves to the decision-making process of the managers of the firm, which includes the accountability of the decision makers for the actions of the firm. The book discusses capturing the intangible impact of the firm's culture through its human resource decision and strategic planning process. The book concludes with an examination of global ethical issues related to environmental sustainability and the developing world.

By embracing a practical approach to these topics of study, the *Absolute Essentials of Business Ethics* highlights both the ethical and unethical behaviors of firms through numerous real-life examples including Patagonia, Costco, LVMH, Bill Gates, Muhummad Yunus, Enron, WorldCom, Samsung, Purdue Pharma, Vale Mining, and the COVID-19 crisis. *Absolute Essentials of Business Ethics* will allow readers the opportunity to reflect on their own personal moral compass through the use of ethical dilemmas such as the Trolley and Heinz dilemmas.

In summary, *Absolute Essential of Business Ethics* provides the reader with a practical application to the sometimes enigmatic relationship between business and ethics.

1 The foundations of business ethics

Essential summary

As humans, we live in a world where rules and regulations are the guidance used to determine right from wrong. However, beyond complying with the legal responsibilities of being a respected member of society, individuals must understand what their ethical responsibilities are when making decisions and taking actions.

This introductory chapter explores ethics from a practical philosophical perspective. From explaining what ethics and business ethics are, to explaining why it is important to study ethics, this chapter lays the ethical groundwork for subsequent chapters. Included among other topics in the chapter is how individuals can structure their decision-making process to make ethical decisions.

Both the teleological and deontological frameworks are presented to give an understanding of the philosophical foundation of ethics. The chapter also presents an interesting ethical dilemma involving a runaway trolley. How the reader responds to this dilemma can give insights into the individual's own moral compass. In summary, this chapter gives the reader the opportunity to see how ethics impacts everyone's day-to-day life experiences.

What is ethics?

The ability to be accountable and take responsibly for one's actions is a fundamental tenant of being a human being. To guide the process of our actions, we have established guidelines for what is acceptable and unacceptable behavior in society. Each person's own ethical values determine the ethical behavior of everyone. Therefore, ethics can be defined as the personal values of the individual which are used to interpret whether a specific action or actions are acceptable and appropriate. From a business perspective, business ethics can be defined as the collective values of the employees of the firm in determining whether the actions of individuals within the firm are acceptable and appropriate.

Why study business ethics?

Business ethics is important to study because there will be circumstances where employees may be asked to perform a task or action which could challenge the values and ethical beliefs of the individual. This request creates an ethical dilemma in which it is always uncertain what correct action should be taken by the individual. Therefore, an ethical dilemma occurs when the individual is required to decide which action may or may not be considered ethical by the firm and/or society. Some decisions are not always "black or white" but are considered "gray" in the distinction of the ethical commitment of the decision maker.

An ethical dilemma can often occur when employees are asked to perform a task by their supervisor which could be considered unethical and potentially illegal. A supervisor in an accounting department may ask an accountant to recognize the revenue of a sale by the firm to be recorded in the last day of a quarter when, in actuality, the revenue should be recognized in the following quarter. This can become a common occurrence in firms who are under extreme pressure to demonstrate their short-term financial performance. By recognizing the sale in the "previous" quarter, the firm has artificially reported its results.

The ethical issue is not the sale itself but when it is recognized. The net result is that unethical issues in the workplace can be a cause of concern for the individual and can be considered a common occurrence within the firm. This type of work environment can lead to the individual being more emotional, less effective, and more vulnerable, leading to an acceptance of this type of behavior in order to cope with the decisions that need to be made in this setting. This coping mechanism can lead to the individual rationalizing his or her decisions related to the ethical dilemma.

Rationalization occurs when either the individual tries to convince him/herself or a third party tries to convince an individual that the unethical decision is not a problem. Rationalization phrases can include "It's not a big deal... This is someone else's responsibility... This must be the way these things are done." Rationalization is used to try to convince the conscience of the individual that it is okay to make this decision even though the person's "gut feeling" contradicts that message. Furthermore, the employee's supervisor uses rationalization to manipulate the actions of the employee for the supervisor to achieve his or her desired goal. The behavior of the individual when making an unethical decision is the focus of different types of ethical examinations.

Types of ethical examinations

An examination of issues related to an ethical dilemma is based on descriptive ethics, analytical ethics, and normative ethics. Descriptive ethics is the collection and presentation of the facts related to the unethical actions of the individual. It is during the descriptive stage that the person reviewing the behavior can understand the chronological actions of the individual. Through the collection of facts, the observer does not try to infer why the person made the decisions leading up to the unethical activity. The interpretation of the facts occurs in the second type of ethical examination, analytical ethics.

Analytical ethics can be defined as the ability to understand the reason or reasons why the course of action by the individual took place which could result in unethical consequences. Analytical ethics shifts the focus from how and when the unethical activities occurred to attempting to answer the question "why?" The identification of the motivation behind the unethical actions can facilitate the learning process for the firm to understand the rationale for the employee's actions. The analysis of the unethical actions of the employee would include the identification and interpretation of multiple variables which could have impacted the decision-making process of the firm.

For example, equity theory could explain the unethical behavior of an employee. Equity theory assumes that each employee's efforts generate a certain perceived value to the firm. If employees continue to make the same effort in the workplace, yet the firm is forced to reduce compensation to the employees, the employees will perceive this action as inequitable. Another example is when an employee's perception of the amount of work and effort that the employee performs for his or her job is equal to the amount of effort of other employees who get compensated at a higher financial level.

Alternatively, if the firm fires one employee and transfers the work to another employee without an acceptable adjustment in the remaining employee's salary, the employee will perceive this action as unfair or inequitable. As a result, through rationalization, employees who do not believe they are being treated fairly and in an equitable manner may have a strong incentive to steal money or other resources from the firm. The employee's rationale is that they deserve and are entitled to take resources from the firm to "equal" the unfair balance. An employee may believe that they can take four reams of paper from the supply closet since the firm "owes" the employee additional compensation.

Normative ethics moves beyond the how and why and shifts to what can be done to ensure the unethical behavior does not occur again in the future. Through normative ethics, the firm can develop a prescribed course of action that will guide the employee to focus on ethical behavior. Normative ethics shifts the focus from the past to the future. It gives employees information on what the firm considers are appropriate ethical actions if in the future the same type of scenario occurs again. The normative ethics approach prescribes the desired actions of the employee to address potential ethical issues before these issues occur.

Through the use of normative ethics, the firm can use the root cause of the unethical behavior that was determined in the analytical examination to attempt to ensure that this type of unethical behavior does not occur in the future. If the unethical behavior is based on the employee's belief that he or she had been treated unfairly, the result could be unethical behavior to correct this perceived unfair treatment by the firm.

Enron and ethical examinations

Founded as a natural gas company in 1987, Enron would become what is considered the "gold standard" for unethical behavior. Driven by increasing its stock price, Enron's CEOs Ken Lay and Jeff Skilling would focus on whatever activities were necessary to increase the stock price. This action not only included unethical manipulations of energy markets, but also included providing false and misleading financial information to the public. The top-level executives at Enron enjoyed the financial benefits of a rising stock price.

From 1998 to 2000, the total compensation paid to the top 200 executives at Enron climbed from $193 million to $1.4 billion due to bonuses and stock options. The personal wealth of the executives increased while external stakeholders including the media were unclear as to why the stock price was increasing at such a high rate. In addition, there was confusion about the strategic focus of Enron.

In March 2001, Bethany McLean from *Fortune* asked the simple question of how Enron made its money. The official response from Enron was that it was competing in "wholesale energy operations and services." In reality, Enron was day trading energy contracts and reporting false transactions related to its business dealings. When Enron's Chief Financial Officer (CFO), Andy Fastow, resigned on October 24, 2001, the Securities and Exchange Commission announced it was investigating the financial reporting at Enron. Less than six weeks later, Enron had filed for bankruptcy.

Descriptive examination of Enron

The descriptive examination of the presentation of the facts related to unethical behavior at Enron revealed multiple areas in which Enron's culture supported and rewarded unethical actions by its managers. Enron had manipulated its financial statements, which included the use of complex off-balance sheet transactions. These complicated transactions artificially improved the financial performance of Enron. Evidence had showed that Enron's two CEOs Ken Lay and Jeff Skilling had both sold Enron stock after they knew the stock price was going to collapse. In addition, they continued to publicly and enthusiastically encourage Enron employees to buy more stock for their retirement funds during the same period. When Enron employee Sherron Watkins became a whistleblower and warned others about the unethical behavior at Enron, she was harassed by Enron executives. Enron also hired the accounting firm, Arthur Andersen, to not only be its external auditor, but also a strategy consultant. This hiring of two related departments within the same firm raised numerous red flags about potential conflicts of interest by the auditing firm.

Analytical examination of Enron

To understand the unethical culture at Enron, an analysis is needed of why Ken Lay and Jeff Skilling acted in an unethical manner. Lay and Skilling made it clear to Enron's employees that the employees would be rewarded handsomely if they increased sales and profits. Through a compensation and bonus system where the end was the only thing that mattered and management did not care about the means, Enron condoned unethical behavior by financially rewarding employees for this type of behavior. Through constantly growing its financial performance, Enron executives and employees benefited from an increased stock price.

Both Lay and Skilling stated, even after their convictions, that they had done nothing unethical. Their rationale was that the actions were approved by Enron's external auditor, Arthur Andersen. In addition, Lay and Skilling did not perceive selling their own stock as insider trading since they believed that they were allowed to sell stock at their pleasure. Furthermore, they claimed that it was not unethical to be optimistic about the future growth potential of Enron and its corresponding financial performance even though they had information which contradicted that level of optimism.

Alternatively, an analysis of their actions could conclude that Lay and Skilling knew that their actions were unethical, but they felt they were too smart to ever be caught by the FBI and the Securities and Exchange Commission. Enron's hiring strategy was that it would seek to only hire the top graduates from the top MBA programs in the world. It was from this belief that Enron always felt that they would have the smartest employees in any meeting with any external stakeholders, including customers, suppliers, and the government. Therefore, Enron executives could always find an explanation for their unethical behavior.

Normative description of Enron

It is through normative examination that companies such as Enron can make corrections to suppress this unethical behavior from occurring the future. Unfortunately for the Enron employees who were not involved in the unethical actions, Enron went bankrupt so the employees did not have a second chance.

It is common to point to the firm's Code of Ethics as a reference point to present a normative course of action so that unethical behavior cannot take place. However, this is not the case for Enron. In July 2002, Enron released its 63 pages of Code of Ethics. Therefore, normative tools such as the Code of Ethics are of no use if the executives of the firm just ignore them during the decision-making process.

The collapse of Enron, in part, resulted in the United States Congress passing the Sarbanes-Oxley (SOX) Act in 2002. Based on the unethical actions at Enron, government regulations now have limits on how long external auditors can have the same client, have banned auditing firms from also having the same client for their consulting business, and forced top-level executives including the CEO to disclose any stock transactions within two days. SOX also made requirements to strengthen the power and accountability of the board of directors of the firm to eliminate unethical behavior by the firm.

Philosophical ethical frameworks

There are two major philosophical ethical frameworks which provide a foundation in the study of ethics. The two frameworks are teleological and deontological.

Teleological frameworks

The teleological ethical framework examines the unethical conduct of individuals from the impact of the decisions made by individuals.

The origin of teleological is from the Greek word *telos*, which means fulfillment. Therefore, teleological frameworks examine the results of the ethical or unethical conduct of an individual. The examination of the consequences, both positive and negative, of the actions of the individual is used as a learning tool in fostering an acceptable normative guideline on what should be the appropriate actions of the individual. Teleological frameworks are composed of three components: ethical egoism, utilitarianism, and Sidgwick's dualism.

Ethical egoism

Embraced by philosophers from Plato to Thomas Hobbes, ethical egoism is based on the premise that an individual's self-interests can coincide with ethical behavior. Egoism is derived from the Latin term, *ego*, which refers to one's self. The underlying assumption of ethical egoism is that every individual should have the ability to promote himself or herself and the resulting achievement of individual goals will result in a positive impact rather than negative impact on society.

The challenge for society is individuals may have a different interpretation on how achieving their self-interests have a positive image in society. At one extreme end of a continuum, there are individuals who believe that every action they perform creates an overall positive benefit to society. Based on this belief system, the individual could rationalize that every action should not only be supported but be acknowledged as beneficial to society.

Ethical egoism is a commonly held belief for individuals who fully embrace a capitalist economic system. If individuals are motivated to perform actions due to receiving rewards and other compensation for their actions, this motivation is based on self-interests. As a result, ethical egoism incorporates self-motivation in its belief framework. Therefore, a society based on ethical egoism is beneficial to both the employees and society. The employees win by achieving rewards and acknowledgment for fulfilling their personal objectives and society wins because the consequences of the employees' actions yield positive benefits for society. For those who do not embrace ethical egoism, the argument is made that individuals have certain obligations to society that are generated through the self-interests of the individuals. One of those obligations is to understand and serve the needs of others, which is the basis of utilitarianism.

Utilitarianism

Utilitarianism is based on the belief that the actions of an individual should be based on providing the greatest good to the greatest number of people. Utilitarianism is derived from the term *utility*. The principle of utility refers to how each person's actions accumulate the overall utility of the community. The focus of utilitarianism is the net result of the cumulative actions of all instead of the examining the individual motives that created the decision for their actions.

The underlying belief system related to utilitarianism is that utilitarianism is the only theory that clearly explains benevolent behavior by individuals. From a holistic perspective, utilitarianism acknowledges that individuals can move beyond focusing on their own self-interests in developing a cognitive lens which identifies and serves the needs of others.

A common identified weakness of utilitarianism is that it is extremely difficult or impossible to properly evaluate the effectiveness of utilitarianism due to the inability to identify what would be considered the greatest good for the greatest number of people. Another potential limitation is the belief that while utilitarianism may provide the greatest good for the greatest number of people, does this mean the people that were not provided the greatest good were treated unfairly?

Sidgwick's dualism

Based on Henry Sidgwick's book, *The Method of Ethics*, Sidgwick's dualism would be the middle ground between the continuum of ethical egoism and utilitarianism. The foundation argument of Sidgwick's dualism is serving one's self-interests as well as serving the needs of others. Sidgwick viewed utilitarianism as rational benevolence and as the foundation of any ethical framework.

Sidgwick also explained the value of self-interests in ethical egoism as the individual using prudence in making decisions. Sidgwick argued that both points of view are needed since the decision made by the individual must satisfy the needs of the individual making the decisions, as well as identifying how the decision will impact the needs of others. The individual must be happy personally with the decision and therefore that happiness can be transferred to others who are impacted by the decision. This type of harmony of satisfying the needs of oneself and others through rational benevolence and prudence results in an ethical model which is acceptable to individuals when they are making decisions related to ethical issues.

Patagonia and teleological frameworks

Patagonia, the clothing company, has a strong entrenched commitment to the natural environment. Since 1985, Patagonia has pledged the equivalent of one percent of its annual sales to support environmental organizations globally. Called 1% for the planet, this program by Patagonia has contributed $89 million in cash and in-kind donations that are able to support the funding of these local community initiatives.

Patagonia also offers an environmental internship program for its employees. This program gives its employees the opportunity to work for a local environmental group of their choice for up to two months while still receiving their paycheck and benefits. The small, local community-based environment groups receive the benefit of having a Patagonia employee committed to the natural environment work for them for free for two months. When the Patagonia employees return to work, they describe their experiences to other employees, which further entrenches the proactive environmental belief system at Patagonia.

ETHICAL EGOISM

It is clear that under the ethical egoism framework, Patagonia would not give 1 percent of its sales to environmental groups nor would it "allow" its employees to leave the firm for two months in order to serve a local environmental group. By solely focusing on the self-interests of the individuals, supporters of ethical egoism would consider allowing employees to volunteer with pay as an inefficient use of Patagonia's resources. As a result, this type of program would not be acceptable to those investors who believe that decisions should always be based on self-interests.

UTILITARIANISM

Patagonia's Environmental Internship program can be viewed as a utilitarian-focused program. Due to the positive environmental impact this program has on local communities, this program can provide the greatest good for the greatest number of people. This program allows Patagonia to not only reach out to local communities but also establish a two-way communication channel to benefit both Patagonia and the environmental groups.

SIDGWICK'S DUALISM

While Patagonia's programs can be viewed as utilitarian, the programs can also be incorporated within Sidgwick's dualism framework. As was mentioned in the previous section, Patagonia's programs attempt to positively impact as many people as possible. However, there are also self-interest benefits in these programs. Patagonia can use these programs as marketing tools to differentiate itself in the marketplace. Patagonia's financial commitment to the natural environment can have a significant impact on customers buying its products. In addition, by establishing communication channels with these environmental groups, Patagonia is better able to address the needs of not only these groups, but other customers committed to the natural environment through the development and design of its products.

Deontological frameworks

Deontological frameworks take a different approach than the teleological frameworks. While teleological frameworks evaluate whether or not the result of the decision and action is ethically favorable or not, deontological frameworks focus on the obligation or duty of the individual in order to determine whether the actions by the individual are right or wrong. The Greek word for duty is *deon*, which is the root of the word deontological. The three deontological-based frameworks are: existentialism, contractarianism, and Kant's ethics.

Existentialism

The core belief of existentialism is that the only person that can truly evaluate whether the decision was ethical or unethical is the individual him or herself. It is based on the free will of the person that determines his/her actions and, therefore, that same person should be ultimately responsible in determining whether the decision made was right or wrong ethically. The evaluation of the actions of the individual should be based on the person's own virtues. Therefore, existentialism is based on the belief that each individual has a moral compass and, therefore, is always able to determine whether the actions are ethical or not based on everyone's perspective.

Contractarianism

Social contract theory or contractarianism is based on the belief that every individual has agreed to certain social contracts for the actions and behavior of the individual to be accepted as part of society. The underlying assumption of contractarianism is that individuals agree to the norms and values set by society and, therefore, have a social contract to act in a manner which agrees with those norms and values. These norms and values are imbedded in agreed-upon principles based on fairness. It is through this belief in fairness that society establishes what is considered acceptable and unacceptable behavior of individuals. Fairness also includes the ability of individuals to have a voice in economic and political actions and have their individual rights protected.

Kant's ethics

Immanuel Kant argued that ethical decisions are based on the free will of the individual, which is the basis of existentialism. However, Kant's ethics move beyond this belief by stating that the free will decisions made by the individual need to be converted into a universal will which supports contractarianism. This two-prong approach of ethical obligations bridges the gap between existentialism and contractarianism. The underlying philosophy of Kant's ethics is that everyone in society who has the free will to make the decisions would make the same decision, which supports the view that the decision of the individual should be considered a universal will. The message that Kant was attempting to portray was that if the individual performs unethical actions, those actions would be evaluated negatively by a global society regardless of who is directly impacted by the decision.

WorldCom and deontological frameworks

WorldCom was a major telecommunications company that was founded by Bernie Ebbers. As CEO, Ebbers aggressively expanded WorldCom including the purchase of another major telecommunication company, MCI, in 1997 for $37 billion. Bernie Ebbers started obtaining loans from WorldCom to pay margin calls of his WorldCom stock. A margin call occurs when an individual has bought stock in a firm but has only paid a small percentage upfront, usually 10 percent of the total cost. As long as the stock goes up in price, the broker who sold the stock to the individual does not need any additional payments. However, if the price of the stock falls below a certain price threshold, the broker will demand that the individual contribute additional payment of the stock. Therefore, individuals who have bought stock on "margin" always want the stock price to increase.

When the WorldCom stock price started to fall, Ebbers had to make additional payments. These additional payments created two different, but related, unethical actions. The first was Ebbers' desire to do whatever possible to have the stock continue to go up in price. The second action was that Ebbers had to start borrowing money from WorldCom to pay for the margin calls. Ebbers had borrowed hundreds of millions of dollars from WorldCom to pay for his own personal investments in WorldCom stock.

At one time, Ebbers had owed almost $340 million to WorldCom from stock margin calls. A subsequent investigation found that WorldCom had improperly recorded certain expenses as capital expenditures, which artificially enhanced the reported financial performance. The manipulation of the financial transactions was based on Ebbers and other top executives trying to ensure that the stock price continued to increase.

EXISTENTIALISM

Bernie Ebbers continued to deny that he did anything illegal or unethical, even after he was sentenced to prison. He claimed that he was not aware of any illegal manipulations of the financial statements of WorldCom. Based on the beliefs of existentialism, Ebbers claimed that he is the only person who can truly evaluate his ethical or unethical behavior, and through his cognitive lens he did nothing wrong. His individual interpretation of his actions corresponds to his underlying belief that what he did was correct and acceptable.

CONTRACTARIANISM

By having a charter to operate as a publicly held firm, WorldCom agreed to follow the social norms of society. A critical social norm is to be truthful to all its stakeholders. A stakeholder is any group of people who have a vested interest in the company. Common stakeholders include customers, shareholders, employees, government agencies, suppliers, and local communities. Therefore, it is expected and required for WorldCom to be truthful in its disclosure of its financial information. Using transparency, WorldCom has the responsibility to communicate any problems or issues to its stakeholders as part of its contractual agreement to operate its business in good faith. By violating its social contract related to transparency and truthfulness, WorldCom's actions are not acceptable from a stakeholder and society perspective.

KANT'S ETHICS

Cynthia Cooper, Vice President of Internal Audit at WorldCom, was not informed nor aware of the fraudulent financials that were being ordered by WorldCom's Chief Financial Officer, Scott Sullivan. After Cooper became suspicious of potential wrongdoing, she worked after office hours since she could not trust Scott Sullivan to prove that fraud was being committed. Cooper ignored warnings from Sullivan that she should not get involved in any investigation related to the financial transactions and continued to gather evidence to prove the fraud. Based on her investigation, the multi-billion financial fraud at WorldCom was uncovered. The actions of Cynthia Cooper are an example of Kant's ethics since she assumed that other people would take the same actions if they were faced with the same set of circumstances. It is this universal will that can convince people to become whistleblowers despite the personal risks involved with those actions.

The trolley problem

The trolley problem is an ethical dilemma where there is a potential clash in the appropriate action based on the teleological and deontological ethical frameworks. One version of the trolley problem is that a runaway trolley is heading down the track toward five workers who would be killed if the train keeps its present course. The only way to save the five workers is to pull a switch that would transfer the train to another track which has one worker on it and that worker would die if the train proceeded on this altered path.

The question is what would you do if you had the opportunity to pull the switch and divert the train? From a utilitarian perspective, the correct course of action would be to pull the switch to save five people instead of one person. The result of this action would be the greatest good for the greatest number. However, from a deontological perspective, you have a social contract with society in which you have agreed not to kill an innocent person despite the positive consequences of your action. This may lead to the conclusion that the correct ethical action would be to do nothing to alter the course of the train.

In another version of the trolley problem, the runaway trolley is heading toward five workers who would be killed if the train continues its path. The difference in this scenario is that there is not an alternative track to switch the path of the train. In this scenario, you are at the top of a footbridge watching the train along with the stranger who is physically very large. The only way you can stop the train is if you push the stranger from the bridge into the direct path of the train. The five workers would be saved but the stranger would die. In this scenario, the same outcomes occur but individuals would be more hesitant to push someone into a runaway train to save the lives of others.

The reason why people would be more hesitant to save five in the second scenario is based on the individual being actively involved in physical contact with another person, which ultimately results in the person's death. In the first scenario, the individual plays a more passive role in determining who lives and who dies and can create the rationale based on the utilitarian belief of performing an action for the greater good.

Another difference in the two scenarios is that the decision maker is using a person as a means to an end. People view other people as individuals who have the same rights as everyone else to survive. By pushing the person off the bridge, the person shifts from being a human being to being an object that is needed to stop the train.

The underlying question in the second scenario is why the individual believes he or she has the right to proactively kill one person to save five people. In addition, the second scenario assumes that pushing the person into the tracks would result in saving the five workers. The train could be going at such a great level of speed it would hit the person and still kill the five workers. This potential outcome would not occur in the first scenario.

A future trolley dilemma?

This ethical dilemma of who to save and who should not be saved continues to be debated as new technology advances of self-driving cars and other self-controlled vehicles occur. These concerns are amplified with the continuing development of Artificial Intelligence. For self-driving cars, should the software controlling the operations of the car take actions only to protect the lives of its passengers or should it be programmed to save the greatest number of people?

Artificial Intelligence will generate future ethical dilemmas by asking the same types of questions when a decision must be made that will take the life of a human being. The basis of the eternal conflict can be best understood by examining science fiction writer Isaac Asimov's three laws of robot behavior. The first law is that a robot may not injure a human being or, through inaction, allow a human being to be harmed. The second law is that a robot must obey the orders given by human beings unless those orders conflict with the first law. The third law is that the robot must protect its own survival unless it conflicts with the first or second laws. If Artificial Intelligence is programmed in a way to address these three laws, the trolley problem would continue to be an ethical challenge for both robots and humans.

Bibliography

Crockett, Molly. 2016. The Trolley Problem: Would You Kill One Person to Save Many Others? *The Guardian*. December 12.

Gallko, Amy. 2015. How to Speak up about Ethical Issues at Work. *Harvard Business Review*. June 4.

Goodpaster, Kenneth E. 1983. *Ethical Frameworks for Management*. Boston, MA: Harvard Business School.

Patagonia Web Site. www.patagonia.com/one-percent-for-the-planet.html; www.patagonia.com/environmental-internship-program.html

Saige, Christoph. 2017. Asimov's Laws Won't Stop Robots from Harming Humans, So We've Developed a Better Solution. *Scientific American*. July 11.

Stanwick, Peter A. and Sarah D. Stanwick. 2016. *Understanding Business Ethics*. Third Edition. Thousand Oaks, CA: Sage Publications.

2 Stakeholders and corporate social responsibility

Essential summary

Just as no person is an island, no firm can effectively serve the needs of others if it just focuses on its own self-interests. In the past, the conventional view of the responsibility of the firm was to solely satisfy the needs of its shareholders. A more current and relevant focal point of all firms is to identify and serve the needs of all the entities that have a vested interest in the operations of the firm. These entities are called stakeholders since they have a "stake" in how the actions of the firm can impact them both today and in the future.

This chapter focuses on the interconnectedness of stakeholders and corporate social responsibility. From the identification of the firm's stakeholders, the chapter transitions to linking those stakeholder connections with the firm's ability to identify and support corporate social responsibility commitments. The cornerstone of the theory of corporate social responsibility is the pyramid created by Archie Carroll, which focuses on how each level can have different impacts on the firm's relationship with its stakeholders. The chapter concludes with an explanation of how and why the firm's corporate reputation is so critical to build and protect its relationship with its stakeholders. In summary, Chapter 2 identifies why it is important for firms to understand the relationship with its stakeholders and how that relationship can have a positive impact on its self-interest goals, as well as serving its altruistic goals.

What is a stakeholder?

A stakeholder can be defined as any individual or group that has a vested interest in the operations of the firm. Since the decisions and actions of the firm impact various groups, these group have a stake in the firm's interactions. Traditional stakeholders for a firm include employees, customers, shareholders, suppliers, governments, local communities, society, and non-governmental organizations (NGOs).

The origins of modern stakeholder theory can be traced back to the Great Depression. In 1931, A.A. Berle argued that since the managers of a firm are responsible for the investment made by the shareholders, the shareholders are the only truly important stakeholders. The managers have been given the power and the authority to maximize the return of the investment by the shareholders. Therefore, it is the fiduciary duty of the managers to make decisions that will yield optimal financial performance. This fiduciary duty is based on the beliefs of agency theory. The tenets of agency theory are that managers are "agents" of the shareholders and, therefore, are legally required to make decisions that best serve the needs and wants of the shareholders. The shareholders are the principals who give the power to the managers to make decisions related to the operations of the firm in exchange for ensuring the decisions coincide with the wishes of the shareholders.

The following year, E. Merrick Dodd made his rebuttal to Berle, stating that all stakeholders are important and not just the shareholders. Dodd argued that Berle's claims are too narrow and that is it not effective for firms to ignore other stakeholders. Firms need to understand that their responsibilities are not just to shareholders, but that firms have obligations to their communities, employees, and consumers. In addition, if firms ignore the governments in which they have operations, there can be significant financial penalties to both the firm and the individuals making unethical and potentially illegal decisions. Dodd highlights that when a firm is incorporated, the firm agrees that its purpose is to serve both shareholders and society.

The debate surrounding who firms should be accountable to resurfaced in 1970. Nobel Prize economist Milton Friedman re-emphasized Berle's belief that firms should only focus on their shareholders and their social responsibility is to ensure the managers make decisions which increase profits for the firm. Friedman argued that a free market system allows individuals to make their own decisions on how to spend their money. Friedman also argued that it is not the responsibility of the firm to determine what social causes to pursue in the name of the shareholders. For its employees, the firm has the responsibility to motivate the employees to make as much money as possible within the legal rules and ethical customs of society.

In 1984, Edward Freeman re-iterated Dodd's argument that all stakeholders are important, and their needs must be satisfied by the firm. By focusing on all the firm's stakeholders, Freeman stated that firms need to take a holistic viewpoint to effectively address the needs of the stakeholders.

It can be argued that serving the needs of all the stakeholders is not mutually exclusive to serving the needs of the shareholders. By serving the needs of the customers, the firm increases its financial performance. By serving the needs of the employees, the employees increase their productivity and potentially decrease the level of employee turnover which, in turn, increases financial performance. By serving the needs of its suppliers, the firm will receive preferential treatment by the suppliers, which can enhance the competitive advantage of the firm and increase its financial performance. By serving the needs of local, national, and foreign governments, the firm does not incur legal liability and protects its corporate reputation, which does not reduce the financial performance of the firm. By serving the needs of the local community, the firm establishes long-term relationships in which the local residents are proud and loyal to the firm in future situations.

How Costco serves its stakeholders

Costco Wholesale Corporation is a global chain of member-based wholesale retailers which provides brand-name merchandise at lower prices than other retail outlets. With sales of $149.4 billion in 2019, Costco has operations in the United States, Canada, Australia, Japan, the United Kingdom, Spain, Mexico, Korea, Taiwan, Iceland, and France. Costco has approximately 100 million members globally and employs 243,000 full and part-time employees. Costco is an excellent example of the challenges a firm faces in addressing the complex needs of various stakeholders. Costco's overall corporate strategy is a single business focusing on selling merchandise through a wholesaler retailer channel.

While its corporate strategy is one dimensional, its approach to its stakeholders is multidimensional. The traditional Costco member may not realize the breadth and depth of Costco's actions related to fulfilling the needs and expectations of its stakeholders. While these actions may be "hidden" to many of its 100 million members, the actions represent Costco's true commitment in embracing its sustainable relationship with its stakeholders. One of the frameworks that Costco uses in its relationship with its stakeholders is its Code of Ethics. The Costco Code of Ethics is based on the philosophy of obeying laws, taking care of its members, taking care of its employees, respecting its suppliers, and rewarding its shareholders.

Addressing the needs of the employees

Costco seeks to provide competitive wages and benefits to its employees. To foster employee loyalty, minimize employee turnover, and maximize employee productivity, Costco provides generous benefits including affordable healthcare coverage and contributions to employees' company-sponsored retirement plans. Costco also provides twice-annual bonuses for employee who have a long tenure working at Costco.

Costco embraces promoting employees from within the firm to encourage employee motivation and loyalty. Over 70 percent of its warehouse managers started their careers at Costco as hourly employees. Men and women at Costco who perform substantially similar work are paid within 99.9% of each other after adjustment due to factors such as the employee's job, company seniority, and hours worked.

Addressing the needs of the community

Costco allocates 1 percent of its pretax profits to selected charitable contributions, which focus on programs related to children, education, and health and human services. In 2018, Costco contributed over $39 million to programs which included United Way, Children's Miracle Network Hospitals, Costco educational scholarships, and disaster relief. Costco also partnered with New Eyes to have Costco members donate used eyewear and hearing aids, which are sorted by New Eyes to be repackaged and distributed to people in need globally. Costco also donated over 34 million pounds of food and provided a cash contribution of $1.75 million in 2018 to the Feeding America food donation program.

Addressing the needs of environmental sustainability

Costco's warehouse design is based on being energy-efficient, sustainable, and environmentally responsible. The designs are consistent with the requirements of the Leadership in Energy and Environmental Design (LEED) program. The Costco buildings use recycled materials including prefabricated structural steel, insulation, and concrete and asphalt for the parking lots. Other environmental initiatives include sustainable landscaping, energy from solar power and fuel cells, sustainable methods for refrigerant management, and comprehensive water management systems.

Addressing the needs of the suppliers and customers

Costco has developed an exclusive private-label brand called Kirkland Signature. As a result, Costco can control each step in the supply chain process, which allows Costco to guarantee its customers that these products are based on sustainability and humane practices, and are respectful to the environment. The sustainability of its food products is based on the monitoring process which is used to ensure that the food has been produced, grown, harvested, processed, transported, and packaged in an environmental sustainable manner. The traceability of its food products allows Costco to guarantee the quality and safety of its food products. Costco embraces a fair trade approach in giving a fair price to the farmers who grow the produce it sells.

Addressing the needs in the protection of human rights

Costco demands its suppliers to agree to follow the requirements established in the Costco Supplier Code of Conduct. This global code applies to all suppliers and was derived from policies, standards, and conventions of the United Nations and the International Labor Organization. The Costco Supplier Code of Conduct protects the human rights and safety of the people who produce, process, and/or harvest the products sold by Costco while understanding the unique cultural and legal differences in countries globally. The Costco Supplier Code of Conduct includes issues such as forbidding human trafficking, the use of fair trade, forbidding the use of minerals which come from conflict areas, and embracing the responsible labor initiative. Costco also has stringent policies for its suppliers related to the welfare and proper handling of all animals used in the production of products sold at Costco. The underlying credo of the handling of animals is based on the Five Freedoms of Animal Well Being. The five freedoms are: freedom from fear; freedom from discomfort; freedom from thirst and hunger; freedom to exhibit natural behavior; and freedom from pain and suffering.

Corporate social responsibility

Corporate social responsibility can be defined as the obligation that firms have in the development and implementation of courses of action which support social issues that are beneficial to society. The obligations of the firms are based on their commitment to fulfill their legal responsibility, their fiduciary responsibility, and responsibility to ensure stakeholders view actions and intentions as legitimate in serving the needs of the stakeholders. Firms can use their corporate social responsibility commitment to differentiate themselves in the marketplace. Using corporate social responsibility initiatives, the firms present evidence as to how their actions support the interests of stakeholders.

There are four reasons why firms should incorporate corporate social responsibility into their strategic focus: moral obligation, sustainability, license to operate, and corporate reputation. The firm's moral obligation is based on the belief that being a positive corporate citizen is the right thing to do as it interacts with its stakeholders. Sustainability is the ability of the firm to provide environmental and community leadership to better serve the needs of the stakeholders. The firm's license to operate refers to the legal right of the firm to operate its business by the government, the community, and other stakeholders. By participating in corporate social responsibility initiatives, the firm can positively enhance its corporate reputation, which can strengthen its ability to differentiate itself, yielding a stronger competitive advantage for the firm.

The corporate social responsibility pyramid

Archie Carroll created the seminal framework to understand how firms address corporate sustainability issues. Commonly called the CSR pyramid, Carroll argues that the firm's comprehensive corporate social responsibilities are based on its economic, legal, ethical, and philanthropic responsibilities.

Economic responsibilities

At the foundation of the pyramid, the firm must be profitable to survive in the long term. The firm was created to generate economic value. The execution of CSR is useless if the firm enters bankruptcy due to poor economic performance. The firm is responsible for using the resources it has available to produce goods and services for society. It is through the generation of economic value that the firm can support the other three corporate social responsibilities.

Legal responsibilities

Above the economic responsibilities in the pyramid is the firm's legal responsibilities. The firm must obey the laws and regulations that are related to its operations. Firms are expected to fulfill their economic obligations while maintaining that their actions are within the boundaries established by laws and government regulations. These obligations include compliance with all local, state, federal, and international regulations, and abiding by all domestic and international laws in which the firm has operations. The minimum requirement of all firms, regardless of the industry in which they compete, is to fulfill their economic and legal obligations. Every firm must generate profits and abide by all applicable laws and regulations.

Ethical responsibilities

The firm's ethical responsibilities can change over time since society's perspective of ethical behavior can change. As a result, ethical responsibilities can be difficult to define and can be customized, in part, based on the ethical values of the managers of the firm. However, ethical responsibilities move beyond matching behavior based on legal responsibilities. The ethical responsibilities of the firm are designed to be integrated in the decision-making process. By incorporating its ethical beliefs into the decisions and actions of the firm, managers can differentiate the strategic focus of the firm to highlight activities which are unique to the firm. This type of differentiation allows the firm to enhance its competitive advantage. One significant advantage of focusing on ethical instead of legal responsibilities is that the firm has more flexibility and control over its actions. If the firm relies on the legal standard as the ethical standard, it is relying on third-party government decision makers to determine what is ethical and what is unethical for the firm. It can match its ethical actions with the acceptable social norms related to that specific type of behavior.

For example, the legal age of employment in Bangladesh is 14 and children work an average of 64 hours per week. The Bangladesh government also allows 12 and 13-year-old children to perform "light work" for up to 42 hours per week. These children earn less than $2 a day. Therefore, it is legal for a multinational corporation to outsource its production to a manufacturing facility in Bangladesh which employees 12-year-old children. While this decision is legal, the stakeholders for the firm would ask whether this decision was ethical.

Philanthropic responsibilities

Philanthropic responsibilities are at the pinnacle of the pyramid. This action moves beyond ethical responsibilities by considering how the firm can directly benefit society beyond the actions of its operations. Firms can identify charitable operations to make financial and non-financial commitments or could provide additional benefits such as day care facilities for employees. Firms can also make a contribution to the arts such as museums, science centers, and theaters. The philanthropic actions of the firm need to be in a manner which is consistent with the charitable and philanthropic expectations of society. It is through these philanthropic initiatives that the firm not only can develop stronger links with its stakeholders, but it gives the firm the opportunity to "give back" to society based on successful financial performance.

Samsung's use of the corporate social responsibility pyramid

Within a month of Samsung's launch of its Galaxy Note 7 smartphone in September 2016, 2.5 million phones had to be recalled due to the threat that the phones would catch on fire. By October 2016, Samsung had permanently discontinued the Galaxy Note 7 smartphone. A primary error caused by Samsung was rushing the Galaxy Note 7 to market to beat the launch of the Apple iPhone 7. As a result, there were design defects in the phone which made the phones vulnerable to exploding and catching fire. The cause of the explosion and/or fire was due to the design of the lithium-ion batteries which power the phone. Lithium-ion batteries are used in electronic devices since they can be quickly recharged without wearing out the battery and at an accelerated rate. However, lithium-ion batteries can also be very volatile and potentially flammable due to the potential chemical reactions occurring within the battery if the battery is not designed correctly.

This type of corporate crisis demonstrates both the flaws when a firm does not follow the pyramid of corporate social responsibility and, subsequently, how a firm can recover its relationship with its stakeholders by effectively using the CSR pyramid framework.

The corporate social responsibility pyramid and the Galaxy Note 7 crisis

ECONOMIC RESPONSIBILITIES DURING THE CRISIS

Samsung created its own crisis, in part, due to its economic responsibilities. Samsung was in a fierce competitive battle with Apple in attempting to acquire a larger global market share. As a result, Samsung's managers forced its engineers to complete the design and production of the Galaxy Note 7 smartphone before the product was ready to sell to the public. By rushing the product to market, the Galaxy Note 7 was sold to the public with a fundamental design flaw. The design of the battery needed to power the Galaxy Note 7 was thinner than previous models. A lithium-ion battery contains positive and negative electrodes. The separation of these electrodes is critical to ensure the phone does not burn or explode. A small piece of material called a separator keeps both the positive and negative electrodes separate. The design of the Galaxy Note 7 required an exceptionally thin battery, which resulted in an exceptionally thin separator. As a result, a microscopic flaw in the separator resulted in the phone catching on fire. In addition, Samsung demanded higher power levels of the battery, which increased the intensity of the fire and/or explosion if both types of electrodes interacted with each other.

ECONOMIC RESPONSIBILITIES AFTER THE CRISIS

The financial implications of the crisis were significant for Samsung. It is estimated that the total cost of the global recall and discontinuation of the Galaxy Note 7 to Samsung was $5.3 billion. Samsung was able to change its strategic focus related to corporate social responsibility and this adjustment yielded strong financial results. By July 2017, Samsung had announced its largest ever quarterly profit due in large part to the introduction of the replacement of the Galaxy Note 7 smartphone. The Galaxy S8 smartphone was an immediate hit with customers who liked its sleek design and larger screen than its competitors. The Galaxy S8 and Galaxy S8+ outsold the Galaxy Note 7 globally.

LEGAL RESPONSIBILITIES DURING THE CRISIS

From the beginning of the crisis, Samsung was reluctant to take full responsibility for the crisis. When the Galaxy Note 7 was first introduced to Korean customers in August 2016, and almost immediately after the product launch, one of the Korean news agencies reported that there were five cases of the smartphones catching on fire. Samsung did not immediately respond and the Korean consumer-safety watchdog, the Korean Agency for Technology and Standards, had requested more information from Samsung related to the fires. A month later in September 2016, the Federal Aviation Administration (FAA) in the United States recommended that passengers boarding airplanes should not bring the Galaxy Note 7 on board with them. The following day, the Consumer Product Safety Commission in the United States urged consumers not to buy Galaxy Note 7 smartphones. Samsung was ignoring its legal obligation to provide a safe product which would not endanger either its users or other individuals.

LEGAL RESPONSIBILITIES AFTER THE CRISIS

Samsung realized that standard operating procedures of the production of its smartphones needed to be changed to guarantee the safety of customers and its compliance with government regulations. Samsung opened its operations to third-party auditors and hired additional researchers and engineers to develop a new quality-controlled-based production system. It announced that it had established a quality assurance program along with other features and developed an eight-point battery safety check to ensure its smartphones would not catch fire in the future. Samsung announced that it was also going to redesign the smartphones to allow more space inside the phone for the battery.

ETHICAL OBLIGATIONS DURING THE CRISIS

Samsung did not follow the traditional ethical and social norms related to its reaction to the Galaxy Note 7 crisis. As was stated in the legal obligations, Samsung is ethically bound to produce a product that is safe to use and is expected to immediately recall and correct any defective products if the product is a potential safety hazard to its customers. When Samsung received the first reports of problems with the Galaxy Note 7, Samsung was very slow to react to the crisis. The company initially only recalled 2.5 million smartphones and told its customers to stop using them and trade the smartphones in for another phone. However, Samsung also announced that it had developed a software update which would limit the amount of charge of the Galaxy Note 7 smartphones. The software would limit the battery charge to 60 percent to reduce the probability of it overheating and catching on fire. This created a confusing mixed message from Samsung about what consumers should do with their phones. Samsung also offered replacement batteries for the smartphones but there were occasions in which the replacement batteries were also faulty.

A major ethical problem for Samsung was its corporate culture. The decisions at Samsung came from the senior executives without any input from the lower level employees. This centralized approach created a climate in which the employees were told just to follow the orders given by the senior executives. Therefore, the Samsung engineers who understood the design problems and the resulting crisis were not allowed to inform the senior managers of the challenges and dangers of the flawed product design. Even during the crisis, the senior managers at Samsung told the engineers to prevent all communications from being transmitted through "official" channels. The result of this "radio silence" was that inconsistent and inaccurate information was occurring between the decision makers in senior management and the engineers who were trying to correct the problem.

ETHICAL RESPONSIBILITIES AFTER THE CRISIS

Samsung realized that its centralized-based culture needed to be adjusted to prevent a future crisis. Samsung focused on its drive for innovation in all its business segments as an umbrella theme to help shape the decisions made by executives. This theme also resulted in the development of a supporting culture in which change was accepted and encouraged.

PHILANTHROPIC RESPONSIBILITIES DURING THE CRISIS

Samsung had failed in its responsibilities of being a good global corporate citizen. Samsung was slow to react to changes and did not understand how its reactive behavior potentially threatened millions of customers. By ignoring the warning signs from its stakeholders, Samsung provided a weak communication channel for those who had a vested interest in its operations. When Samsung ignored the initial warnings, consumers went to social media and published photos, videos, and testimonials of the problems they had with the Galaxy Note 7 smartphone.

PHILANTHROPIC RESPONSIBILITIES AFTER THE CRISIS

Samsung also realized that it did not have proper communication channels with its stakeholders during the crisis. As a result, Samsung became more aggressive in monitoring the information presented on social media as well as the overall consumer sentiment for its smartphones. By the end of 2017, Samsung had moved from seventh to sixth place in the Best Global Brands list and Samsung brand valuation had increased by 9 percent.

On October 26, 2017, almost exactly one year after the Galaxy Note 7 crisis started, Samsung announced that it would re-introduce its annual Samsung Charity Gala in New York. Samsung also announced its philanthropic platform called Samsung Gives, which includes community programs for youth, homelessness, veterans, financial literacy, and entrepreneurship programs. Tim Baxter, CEO and President of Samsung Electronics North America, stated that: "At Samsung, every day we are inspired by the people who are helping to build a better world, but especially this year, those who are out there lending a hand to those who need to rebuild their communities and their lives."

Ethics and corporate reputation

A strong positive corporate reputation not only serves an emotional goal of the managers of the firm, but it can be paramount in enhancing the firm's competitive advantage. A seminal part of the perspective of the firm's stakeholders is the determination of the firm's reputation. When the reputation is moving along a favorable path, this will further address the needs and expectations of the stakeholders.

For example, individuals will ask friends, colleagues, and even go on evaluation-based websites to determine which plumber to use or which lawn service is the best value. These recommendations are based on the previous experience the individual has had with the firm, which forms the basis of the individual's reputation to perform the promised service in a satisfactory manner. This individual reputation provides the same value to the individual as a firm's corporate reputation provides for the firm. Stakeholders want to interact with firms that have a positive corporate reputation and will shun firms that have a negative corporate reputation. Therefore, a firm's corporate reputation is based on its strategy, corporate cultures, and values that are perceived from its stakeholders.

A firm can validate its strong positive reputation through producing products that are safe and dependable, having a work environment that supports and motivates its employees, and being able to succeed in both its financial and non-financial goals. As a result, a firm's reputation is a vehicle it can use to communicate its values and beliefs for serving the needs of its stakeholders. The firm's reputation is an intangible asset which can yield long-term competitive advantage. This advantage is obtained from not only serving the needs of the stakeholders but by differentiating itself from other firms, which enhances its ability to create brand loyalty through the customers.

This positive relationship with stakeholders allows the firm to develop a halo effect. A halo effect occurs when the reputation of a firm can distort the perception of the firm's actions by its stakeholders. The firm's stakeholders judge negative actions less harshly when the firm has a positive reputation. Alternatively, the stakeholders of a firm with a negative halo effect will stress the importance of negative actions by the firm to "prove" their negative perception of the firm.

Purdue Pharma: How a negative corporate reputation led to bankruptcy

On September 15, 2019, Purdue Pharma filed for Chapter 11 bankruptcy. Purdue, the maker of the opioid OxyContin, was facing over 2,600 federal and state lawsuits pertaining to its activities related to the marketing and distribution of OxyContin. OxyContin is a highly addictive drug and is considered to be the foundation drug of the opioid crisis occurring globally. Court documents revealed that Purdue executives knew that OxyContin was more dangerous to the patients than what Purdue told the doctors prescribing the drug. Internal documents also stated that one of the goals of the Purdue sales representatives was to increase the number of patients that used OxyContin, including veterans and vulnerable seniors. Additional documentation revealed that Purdue executives were aware of the risks related to the opioid epidemic and did nothing in response to that information.

As a result, Purdue Pharma had developed a negative halo effect in which the release of internal documents supported the underlying beliefs of its stakeholders that Purdue was not only profiting from the opioid crisis but was a dominant factor in the creation and maintenance of the crisis. This perspective by Purdue's stakeholders became entrenched in the beliefs of its stakeholders. As a result, through pressure from the government, consumers, the media, and society for Purdue to stop producing and promoting OxyContin, Purdue's negative corporate reputation accelerated its downward spiral until it was forced to file for bankruptcy.

Bibliography

Associated Press. 2016. Samsung Galaxy Note 7 Recall to Cost at Least $5.3 Billion. *Los Angeles Times.* October 14.

Beaubien, Jason. 2016. Study: Child Laborers in Bangladesh Are Working 64 Hours a Week. *NPR.org.* December 7.

Berle, Adolf A. 1931. Corporate Powers as Powers of Trust. *Harvard Law Review.* 44:7. 1049–1074.

Carroll, Archie. 1991. The Pyramid of Corporate Social Responsibility: Toward the Moral Management of Organizational Stakeholders. *Business Horizons.* 34:4. 39–48.

Costco Website. https://investor.costco.com/corporate-profile-2; https://mobile content.costco.com/live/resource/img/sustainability-archive/2018-sustainability-archive.pdf

Dodd, Merrick E., Jr. 1932. For Whom Are Corporate Managers Trustees? *Harvard Law Review.* 45. 1365–1372.

Dolcourt, Jessica. 2017. Samsung Galaxy Note 7 Recall: Here's What Happens Now. *Cnet.com.* April 16.

Dowling, Grahame. 2004. Corporate Reputations: Should You Compete on Yours? *California Management Review.* 46:3. Spring. 19–36.

Dua, Tanya. 2017. From a 'Cultural Meme' to a Comeback Kid: How Samsung Overcame Its Galaxy Note 7 Fiasco. *Business Insider.* October 6.

Fombrun, Charles. 1996. *Reputation: Realizing Value from the Corporate Image.* Boston, MA: Harvard Business Press.

Freeman, R. Edward 1984. *Strategic Management: A Stakeholder Approach.* Boston, MA: Pitman.

Friedman, Milton. 1970. The Social Responsibility of Business Is to Increase Its Profits. *New York Times Magazine.* September 13.

Hoffman, Jan and Mary Williams Walsh. 2019. Purdue Pharma, Maker of OxyContin, Files for Bankruptcy. *The New York Times.* September 15.

Martin, Timothy W. and Eun-Young Jeong. 2017. Samsung Posts Record Profits on Back of Strong Galaxy S8 Sales. *The Wall Street Journal.* July 26.

Pabla, Navreet. 2019. Pharma Companies Struggling to Maintain Reputation. *Healthcare Weekly*. March 21.

Samsung website. https://news.samsung.com/us/samsung-2017-charity-gala-community-commitment/

Stanwick, Peter A. and Sarah D. Stanwick. 2016. *Understanding Business Ethics*. Third Edition. Thousand Oaks, CA: Sage Publications.

Stanwick, Peter A. and Sarah D. Stanwick. 2018. Samsung's Galaxy Note 7: How a New Product Launch Can Go Up in Smoke. *International Journal of Education and Social Science*. 5:11. 22–25.

3   Leadership and corporate governance

Essential summary

A leader has valuable abilities to guide a firm through both crises and triumphs. While the leader can inspire and motivate others, the leader must also be cognizant of his or her influence on the behavior of others. This behavior must be consistent with the ethical expectations of one of the firm's most important stakeholders, the board of directors. The foundation of this chapter is to examine the ethical responsibilities of leaders and the corporate governance system of the firm, which is proxied by examining the firm's board of directors. The chapter dives into the debate of the comparative effectiveness of transactional and transformational leaders and includes a comparison of the leadership styles of Bill Gates and Reed Hastings. For corporate governance, the chapter presents a reflection of what are the duties of the board of directors as well as why it is so difficult for some boards to remain ethically driven in their decision-making process. The chapter continues with a discussion of possible conflicts of interest related to the board of directors, which asks the hypothetical question of why shareholders would tolerate such actions by its board members. The equally potential unethical action of skyrocketing CEO compensation is also discussed in the chapter with rationales given from a philosophical perspective.

Ethical leadership

To be an effective manager, an individual must also be an effective leader. A critical attribute of an effective manager is being able to incorporate ethical values in his or her leadership capabilities. Ethical leadership can be defined as a manager who demonstrates normatively appropriate conduct through his/her personal actions and who is able to promote this type of conduct to other employees through communication, reinforcement, and decision making that emphasizes strong ethical value. A positive outcome of strong ethical leadership is the creation and maintenance of a positive ethical work climate for the employees of the firm.

A positive ethical work climate is critical in order to establish an ethical foundation in which the employees have a supportive work environment which leads to higher levels of employee satisfaction, commitment, and motivation. Ethical leadership creates an atmosphere that encourages the development of role models within the firm which demonstrate the desired behaviors of the employees. Employees will observe the behaviors and actions of their managers to obtain a clear understanding of what the manager considers to be appropriate and inappropriate. Much like a child observing the behavior of a parent, employees want to be rewarded for their behavior and will examine the behavior of the manager in order to enhance their ability to perform to the expectations of the manager.

This results in a "trickle down" effect of ethical leadership in which management at each level has been able to demonstrate ethical leadership attributes and those attributes are mimicked by managers and employees at lower levels within the firm. The ability to encourage ethical leadership by managers allows the employees to believe that they are performing their tasks both effectively and ethically, which leads the employees to believe that they are valuable resources and to make significant contributions to the overall performance of the firm.

Characteristics of ethical leadership

To effectively manage the firm and effectively manage the ethical values within any organization, a manager must be an effective leader. Managers have two different types of leadership styles which can be used to establish and maintain the ethical values of the employees. These leadership styles are transactional and transformational leadership.

Transactional leadership

A transactional leadership style is one in which the manager motivates the employee through the mutual benefit of an agreed-upon transaction between the two parties. For example, a manager could offer an employee a $500 bonus if the employee completes a critical time-sensitive assignment by a specific deadline. The employee is rewarded for completing the assignment within the agreed time frame and the manager receives the assignment within the agreed time frame.

It is through this agreement about the transaction that leaders can monitor the activities of the employees and ensure that specific tasks are performed based on specific requirements. These contingent rewards are based on the agreement between the manager and the employee that the reward promised to the employee will be given contingent on the successful completion of the task.

A transactional leadership style limits the ability of the manager to be able to effectively establish an ethical commitment of the employees. By developing activities based on transactions, employees will view each request for action by the manager based on the philosophy of "what is in it for me?" The managers have "trained" the employees to expect to receive rewards for their actions and, therefore, will not perform functions that are outside the realms of their job description. As a result, employees will not view actions from an ethical standpoint but instead will view these actions from a self-interest viewpoint.

FOUNDER OF MICROSOFT, BILL GATES: TRANSACTIONAL LEADER

The founder of Microsoft, Bill Gates, used transactional leadership as the CEO of Microsoft to focus on its global growth. Gates focused on short-term results and used the monitoring and controlling mechanisms available to him as CEO to ensure that the actions of the employees corresponded with his expectations. Gates had built, within Microsoft, the necessary formalized structures and systems that would reward the employees for their actions. By focusing on short-term goals, Gates expected the employees to complete their tasks without allowing them the flexibility to experiment on projects that were outside of their job responsibilities. Gates oversaw the product strategy at Microsoft and did not ask for, nor expect, employees' creativity in the product design. The creative process was solely Gates' responsibility. Gates was a task-oriented leader at Microsoft who thrived on conflict and would challenge his employees to defend their decisions. Gates believed that his vision should not be interrupted by input from its employees and he did not need anyone to tell him how to run Microsoft.

Therefore, the primary function of the manager in this type of leadership style is the ability to be able to monitor the actions of the employees instead of inspiring the employees to perform actions beyond what is expected of them in their job descriptions. The inspiration of the firm's employees can be executed through a transformational leadership style.

Transformational leadership

In contrast with transactional leadership, a transformational leader is one who focuses on the development and implementation of a long-term strategic vision. A transformational leader is charismatic in nature, which allows the leader to effectively convey the ethical values and ideals to his/her employees through various communication mediums. This leadership style allows the leader to not only motivate employees, but also challenge employees to grow from both a personal and career perspective through the leader's inspiration.

By inspiring the employees, the employees understand their roles and expectations within the firm. Therefore, the employees know and accept the ethical values of the leader and do not need to refer to policies or manuals in order to determine what is "right and wrong." This gives the employees the freedom to develop their own ideas in an autonomous setting in which creativity and innovation thrive within the guidelines established by the ethical values of the firm.

Furthermore, since the actions of the employees are not based on contingent rewards through transactions, the employees develop strong altruistic value systems in which the employees will perform functions beyond their job descriptions to the betterment of other employees and the firm. It is through transformational leadership that employees are encouraged to be innovative and creative in developing new projects which will be beneficial to the firm.

As a result, a transformational leadership style allows the leader to inspire and develop an ethical commitment among employees as well as provide clarity and holistic meaning to the goals of the expectations. A transformational leader also "rewards" the employees by encouraging the development of both personal and career-based goals, which increases the level of commitment and loyalty the employees have with the firm. This results in highly motivated and dedicated employees who are least likely to leave the firm because the firm can satisfy all the goals of the employees. In addition, the highly positive work climate that is created and protected by a transformational leader encourages employee loyalty, which also reduces the threat of employees leaving the firm.

FOUNDER OF NETFLIX, REED HASTINGS: TRANSFORMATIONAL LEADER

As a pioneer of online streaming of movies, Reed Hastings embraced a transformational leadership style in this disruptive industry. Hastings started Netflix by mailing DVD movies to customers but realized that the industry had evolved into serving its customers by providing access to movies online. Hastings realized that Netflix's employees needed to be able to quickly adapt to industry changes and, therefore, created a human resource model in which formal reviews and bonuses were eliminated. As a transformational leader, Hastings did not have to rely on formalized processes in order to motivate the employees at Netflix.

Through his charismatic leadership, Hastings was able to establish a strong, trusting bond with Netflix's employees and allowed the employees the freedom of having complete autonomy in their ability to make and implement their own decisions. The only guideline established by Hastings was that the decisions made by the employees were based on serving the best interests of Netflix. This leadership style personifies the ability of a firm to have its ethical values engrained in employees' beliefs. The employees at Netflix were acutely aware of what is acceptable and not acceptable from an ethical viewpoint, and that value system was supported by the trust that bonded the employees and the managers at Netflix.

Ethics and corporate governance

Corporate governance can be defined as the system that is implemented by the firm to monitor and formally evaluate the overall operations of the firm. The investors (owners) of the firm expect and demand that managers are accountable for their actions.

As a result, the firm must put in place an evaluation system to assure the owners that the managers are making decisions that are in the best interest of the firm. While initially focusing on the needs of the firm's shareholders, the role of corporate governance has evolved to include evaluating the actions and performance of the firm based on satisfying the needs of all the firm's stakeholders. It is through the evaluation of the firm via the corporate governance framework that stakeholders can determine the firm's ethical commitment based on its actions.

As a result, the stakeholders, not only the shareholders, drive the corporate governance system within the firm. Each stakeholder establishes a set of demands and expectations to evaluate the performance of the firm. While the shareholders focus on the financial performance of the firm, the firm's employees, suppliers, and local communities expect a higher level of integrity in the actions of the firm. The government expects the firm to follow all government laws and regulations while NGOs expect the firm to follow the global standards of ethical performance.

The firm should incorporate stakeholder expectations into its corporate governance system to establish a long-term positive relationship with its stakeholders. The firm must also be aware and include dimensions of global compliance standards in its corporate governance system to ensure that the firm is in global compliance regardless of where its operations are around the world. This global awareness also relates directly to the firm's global image. Once a firm has expanded internationally, its brand name becomes global. Therefore, the firm must be diligent in protecting its image and reputation since unethical activities in one region of the world can have a negative impact on its reputation globally. It is through the corporate governance system that the firm can project its ethical and stakeholder commitment, which can enhance its competitive advantage regardless of where it competes in the world.

Satyam: When lack of corporate governance fails all stakeholders

On January 7, 2009, the founder of Indian IT services firm, Satyam Computers, B. Ramalinga Raju announced that Satyam had been falsifying its financial statements for many years, which included overstating sales and profits by $1 billion. The following day Raju and his brother Rama, who was also a co-founder of Satyam, were arrested and the Indian government dissolved Satyam's board of directors.

Raju had to finally disclose the financial improprieties after the failed attempt by Satyam to invest $1.6 billion into two Raju family-owned properties. The investment was for Maytas Properties and Maytas Infrastructures, which is Satyam spelled backwards. The board of directors at Satyam had approved this investment on December 16, 2008, while ignoring the blatant conflict of interest of the proposed transactions. When the proposed investment was made public by the media, there was an immediate negative reaction due to the lack of corporate governance by the board of directors, which resulted in a significant drop in the stock price. After the announcement, the board of directors reconvened on the same day and cancelled the proposed investment.

By January 9, four board members resigned, including Satyam's non-executive director and three outside independent directors. One of the directors who resigned was M. Rammohan Rao, who was the dean of the Indian School of Business in Hyderabad (ISB). Rao was the chair of both December 16 meetings which involved the conflict of interest investment. On January 8, the day after his resignation, Rao was forced to resign as the dean of ISB.

A key linchpin to the corporate governance system is the verification of the external auditors to the operations of the firm. It is though the confirmation that the firm has performed its operations in a legal manner through the auditing process that the investors are able to have trust in the firm's operations. The auditor for Satyam, PricewaterhouseCoopers, commented that its audits were conducted in accordance with applicable auditing standings and its evaluation of the financial statements of Satyam were supported by appropriate audit evidence. In the aftermath of any publicized corporate fraud, both the firm and the external auditor made allegations against each other. The external auditor accused the firm of not providing the necessary documentation to uncover the fraud and the firm accused the external auditor of not performing the fiduciary due diligence in uncovering the fraud.

From a corporate governance perspective, Satyam's formal monitoring mechanism, its board of directors, failed to perform its primary function of protecting the investment by its shareholders. The failure is highlighted by the lack of accountability of Raju and his brother in making investment decisions that reflected their own personal self-interests instead of those of the firm. Another question that should have been raised in the corporate governance monitoring process was the rationale of a computer company to make investments in real estate and infrastructures not related to its current operations. Since these investments are not part of Satyam's core competences or its business expertise, there should have been challenges from the board of directors as to why that would be the optimal use of an over a billion-dollar investment.

From an individual board member responsibility, under Indian law, a board member may not vote on an investment proposal if he or she is not present at the board meeting where the proposal was discussed. Therefore, while Satyam's non-executive director who subsequently resigned was not eligible to vote on the proposal, he still received approximately $200,000 annually for being a board member of Satyam. The payment was based on the board member's rendering of "professional services."

Board of directors

As shown in the example of Satyam Computers, the board of directors play a critical role in any firm's corporate governance. The board of directors represent the proxy interests of the shareholders. It is through the monitoring actions of the board that shareholders should be assured that their best interests are served by the actions of the managers of the firm. This relationship between the board and the shareholders is based on agency theory. The owners or shareholders are the principals in the relationship and the managers act as agents who execute strategic actions in the best interest of the shareholders.

Board members can be considered to be either inside or outside board members. An inside board member has a direct financial link with the firm and is usually an employee of the firm. An outside board member does not have a direct financial link with the firm. It is expected that each firm would have a combination of both inside and outside board members to properly monitor and evaluate the performance of the firm.

The composition of the board should be based on core ethical values such as honesty, integrity, loyalty, responsibility, fairness, and corporate citizenship. It is through these attributes that shareholders should believe that the board is performing their fiduciary duties for the owners. The board's fiduciary duties are the legal responsibilities the board members have in objectively evaluating the activities and results of the firm's performance. These duties include establishing and maintaining internal financial controls, communicating financial information both internally and externally, evaluating the firm's ethical commitment including its code of ethics, selecting the firm's external auditor, and establishing and revising the firm's different board committees.

Types of board of directors

The passage of the Sarbanes-Oxley Act (SOX) in the United States in 2002 brought significant changes to the role and accountability of board members. In the past, boards could act in a passive way in which they did not offer nor would be asked for input from the management of the firm in corporate-level decisions. After SOX was passed, board members were legally responsible to be active participants in the monitoring the activities of the firm. As a result, there are five different types of board of directors based on their involvement in the decision-making process of the firm. The five types are: passive, certifying, engaged, intervening, and operating. The passive is the least involved type of board while the operating is the most involved type of board.

Passive board

As was previously stated, many boards in the past could play a passive role without significant legal peril. As the least involved type of board, the passive board is known for approving whatever proposals are presented by management. This "rubber stamping" approach to corporate governance is in direct conflict with shareholders' expectations of the actions of the board. It could be argued that not only is this type of board inappropriate, but it is a breach of the board's fiduciary responsibilities.

Certifying board

A certifying board performs the minimal ethical and legal responsibilities as a board. The responsibilities of a certifying board are to ensure that the firm is in compliance with all laws and regulations pertaining to the firm's operations. If there are violations by the firm, the board aids in the development of a course of action to resolve the issue and recommend changes in the firm to ensure that the violations do not occur in the future. A certifying board will draw on the expertise of its outside members to give different perspectives on what adjustments need to be made for future compliance. A certifying board will also develop and maintain a succession process for its board members as well as senior-level executives within the firm.

Engaged board

An engaged board is based on a fundamental shift in the role and expectations of the board of directors. An engaged board plays a proactive role in the decision-making process of the firm by providing advice and support to the firm's management team. This input is invaluable when providing the managers of the firm with additional information from diverse perspectives which allow them to consider different scenarios when making corporate-level decisions. In its role as an advisor, an engaged board will provide externally obtained information which can facilitate the decision-making process of the top-level managers of the firm.

Intervening board

An intervening board takes the participation process one step further by becoming actively involved in all major decisions of the firm. An intervening board is fully committed to helping the top-level managers make optimal decisions which have the greatest positive impact on the firm's stakeholders.

Operating board

The operating board is the most actively involved type of board of directors. The board is involved in making the key decisions for the firm and the management of the firm is responsible for executing these decisions. By embracing the diversity of the skills and knowledge of each board member, the firm can reap the benefits of a multidimensional decision-making process. This type of board structure is rare since the CEO and other top-level managers must be willing to give up power and control to allow others to make the critical decisions for the firm. The CEO must have full trust in the skills and experience of the board for the board to take over control of the decision-making process.

Possible conflicts of interest related to the board of directors

CEO duality

The challenge of deciding the level of management control in the decision-making process can be demonstrated based on the selection of the chairperson of the board. The chairperson has the power to determine the agenda for each board meeting, the ability to select the members of each board subcommittee, and to decide on what information is presented to the board to be used in board meetings. If the CEO is also the chairperson of the board, the CEO has duality due to his or her two responsibilities. CEO duality results in the CEO having enormous power in the decision-making process of the firm.

By being able to control the functioning ability of the board, the CEO can potentially manipulate the board meetings to favor his or her own self-interests. Therefore, if the CEO wanted to make decisions which were to beneficial his/her own self-interests, but not beneficial to the firm, those decisions could be more easily implemented from a CEO duality position. As a result, an unethical CEO may not be constrained if the CEO also has control of the decision-making process of the board. CEO duality could also create ineffective boards who do not have the ability to veto decisions made by the top management team. Previous academic research has shown that firms that have CEO duality consistently underperform compared with firms that do not have CEO duality.

Nomination of board members

The shareholders of the firm vote to determine the board of directors of the firm. While this appears to be a democratic process, the process is set up to favor the firm. The selection of candidates for board membership is developed by the firm, which means there is a very minimal chance of a recommendation made by shareholders reaching the ballot. The board of directors' nominating committee develops the list of candidates, which can create conflicts of interest by appointing board members who are loyal to the CEO and, therefore, will support decisions made by the top management team. Once the board member has been selected, it is very difficult for shareholders to exercise their theoretical power to have the board member removed.

Inside versus outside board members

By their nature of working for the firm, inside board members will have an inherent potential conflict of interest in the decision-making process.

Inside board members will seek decisions which will attempt to serve both their own self-interests as well as the interests of the firm's stakeholders. The underlying foundation of this conflict of interest is that inside board members are inclined to protect themselves and their colleagues when decisions are made at board meetings. This "quid quo pro" philosophy ensures that loyalty of the actions of the inside board will be rewarded when other inside board members need to be protected and defended in future meetings.

Interlocking directorates

Interlocking directorates occur when board members become the link between two firms. For example, the CEO of firm A is on the board of directors of firm B and the CEO of firm B is on the board of directors of firm A. This is an example of interlocking directorates since each CEO is technically an outside board member for the other firm, while in actuality the linkage of the relationships to each other firm creates a potential conflict of interest. In the United States, interlocking directorates is controlled by the Clayton Antitrust Act of 1914. This act prohibits board members from interlocking if the result is the reduction of competition between two rival companies.

For example, in 2009, the Federal Trade Commission (FTC) investigated interlocking directorates related to Google and Apple. Google's CEO, Eric Schmidt and former CEO of Genentech, Arthur D. Levinson were board members of both Google and Apple. The FTC had threatened Google and Apple that they would go to court if the interlocking was not decoupled. The net result was that Arthur Levinson resigned from Google's board and Eric Schmidt resigned from Apple's board. The rationale for Schmidt to be invited to the Apple board in 2006 was to create a common alliance to battle the common enemy of Microsoft. However, within three years, Google's expansion into different technology-based industries resulted in Google becoming more of a potential competitor to Apple instead of a partner. For example, Google introduced Android-based software smartphones in 2007 which competed directly against Apple's iPhones. Other areas in which Google and Apple became competitors included web browsers, photo-editing software, and the distribution of music and video.

Enron's board of directors: The gold standard of unethical behavior

A year before Enron's bankruptcy due to its unethical and illegal activities, Enron's board of directors was recognized as one of the top boards in the

United States based on an evaluation in *Chief Executive Magazine*. In its October 2000 issue, the magazine identified the criteria to be considered an exemplary board with characteristics such as boards having harmony with the CEO and the development and implementation of strategic issues which serve the needs of stakeholders, including local communities. Enron's board also had established a "strong corporate governance" focus and could be considered a role model for other firms on how an effective board should operate.

What was not included in these criteria were the board's numerous conflicts of interest, which included the formation of consulting and other financial agreements with Enron to ensure Enron's top executives had free rein of its operations without any restrictions by the board of directors. Enron's board also suspended the enforcement of its Code of Ethics by allowing Enron's CFO Andy Fastow to create individual externally controlled partnerships with Enron, a direct violation of Enron's policy related to conflict of interest. These partnerships were used to transfer debt from Enron's financial statements and Fastow received over $30 million in exchange for these transactions.

Enron's board members were some of the highest paid in the United States, receiving an average annual compensation of cash and stock of $400,000. Furthermore, various board members received consulting fees from Enron which were not included in their official board compensation package.

Ethics and CEO compensation

A recent study by the Economic Policy Institute published in August 2019 found some startling results related to CEO compensation. The study found that from 1978 to 2018, the average compensation for CEOs in the largest 350 firms in the United States had increased by 940.3 percent yet the increase for the typical worker during that time frame increased by only 11.9 percent. The average pay of the CEOs of the firms in the study for 2018 was $17.2 million with a ratio of 278 to 1 as compared with the typical worker compensation. The 278 to 1 refers to the CEO being paid, on average, 278 times more than a typical worker within the same firm. In 1965, the CEO to worker ratio was 20 to 1 and even by 1989, it had only risen to 58 to 1.

The Economic Policy Institute argues that CEOs are receiving exorbitant pay not due to the level of increased productivity of the firm nor due to the ability to possess extremely valuable specific skills which are in high demand. The Economic Policy Institute states that the underlying reason for the high levels of compensation is the CEO's ability to have the power to determine the compensation levels of the top executives within the firm.

Furthermore, firms can hire compensation consultants in order to facilitate the determination of the compensation of the CEO and other top-level executives. These consultants have an inherent potential conflict of interest since the consulting firms are compensated by the firm. Therefore, the compensation consulting firm wants to establish a long-term relationship with each of its client firms. As a result, the consulting firms have an incentive to recommend high levels of compensation in order to ensure they will be hired by the CEO in the future.

CEO compensation from an ethical philosophical framework

CEOs have used many rationales to justify their level of compensation from the ethical philosophical framework. From Kant's perspective, the CEO could state that everyone would act in a similar fashion by being given the ability to obtain a higher level of compensation as a reward for being a CEO. The conclusion of the CEO may be that this action would be universal in scope so, therefore, it would be considered ethical.

From an ethical egoism perspective, the CEO's compensation level is based on the ability of the CEO to make decisions that have a positive financial impact for the shareholders as well as helping serve the needs of the firm's other stakeholders. The assumption of ethical egoism is that the ability to meet the financial expectations of the firm's shareholders should be rewarded with increased levels of compensation.

From a deontological perspective, CEO compensation could be perceived as being based on the evaluation of the decision-making process instead of focusing on the selection and implementation of the decisions made by the CEO. Therefore, the determination of the compensation is based on the decisions made by the board of directors' compensation committee which evaluates the overall performance of the CEO. This perspective also allows the board of directors and the CEO to defend a high level of compensation even if the firm was not able to optimize its financial performance. By evaluating the decision-making process and not necessarily the consequences of the decision, a potential disconnect is created between evaluation of the CEO and the overall performance of the firm.

From a utilitarian perspective, CEO compensation could be justified based on the ability of the CEO to make decisions which provide the greatest good to the greatest number of people. By presenting a case to demonstrate that the decisions made by the CEO were beneficial to the firm's stakeholders, the CEO can justify his/her level of compensation.

From a relativist perspective, the level of CEO compensation could be considered based on the ability of decision makers to be able to use themselves as well as their peers as a benchmark for the evaluation of ethical standards. Therefore, the commonality of the views of the board and the CEO would support the belief that it would be ethical for the CEO to obtain high levels of compensation.

Bibliography

Anonymous. 2009. *Scandal at Satyam: Truth, Lies and Corporate Governance.* Wharton, PA: University of Pennsylvania. January 9.

Bass, Bernard and Bruce Avolio. 1993. *Improving Organizational Effectiveness Through Transformational Leadership.* Thousand Oaks, CA: Sage Publications.

Bass, Bernard and Paul Steidlmeier. 1999. Ethics, Character, and Authentic Transformational Leadership Behavior. *Leadership Quarterly.* 10:2. 181–218.

Conger, Jay Alden and Rabindra Nath Kanungo. 1998. *Charismatic Leadership in Organizations.* Thousand Oaks, CA: Sage Publications.

Felo, Andrew J. 2011. Corporate Governance and Business Ethics. Ed. Alexander Brink. *Corporate Governance and Business Ethics.* Dordrecht, Germany: Springer. 281–296.

Heckl, Jason. 2019. Leadership Styles: Qualities of a Good Leader. *Strategy Management Consulting.* August 12.

Helft, Miguel. 2009. Google and Apple Eliminate Another Link Tie. *The New York Times.* October 12.

Mishel, Lawrence and Julia Wolfe. 2019. CEO Compensation Has Grown 940% since 1978. *Economic Policy Institute.* August 14.

Nadler, David. 2004. Building Better Boards. *Harvard Business Review.* 82: 102–111.

Stanwick, Peter A. and Sarah D. Stanwick. 2016. *Understanding Business Ethics.* Third Edition. Thousand Oaks, CA: Sage Publications.

4 Strategic planning and culture

Essential summary

The famous heavyweight boxer Mike Tyson once said that "Everyone has a plan until they get punched in the mouth." While managers of a firm never (hopefully) have to experience this action firsthand, it does relate directly to this chapter. This chapter focuses on the ethical aspects of strategic planning. Every manager must have developed a strategic plan which is consistent with the ethical values and vision of the individual and the firm. However, managers also need to be aware that they are responsible for adapting these plans when changes occur either at the formulation or implementation phase of the strategy process. Referring to Mr. Tyson, an effective manager not only develops the initial plan, but recovers and revises the plan in an ethical manner if the circumstances demand it. It is from this lens that the chapter presents the concepts of both strategic planning and culture.

Managers must be able to adjust and make corrections to both strategic planning and the culture of the firm to ensure the long-term sustainability of the firm. This chapter discusses how ethical considerations should be integrated in the decision-making process. The section on emergent strategies is a direct reference for managers to always be alert to capitalizing on new opportunities which were not considered in the planning process.

As with strategic planning, managers must understand the value of a positive, supportive, and thriving corporate culture and the risks and dangers of having a toxic corporate culture. The chapter highlights how important it is for managers to "manage" the culture of their units. While the firm's culture is "intangible," the positive outcomes of a supportive culture and the negative outcomes of a dysfunctional culture can be identified through tangible actions. Therefore, managers have a legal and ethical responsibility to change the culture of their units if the corporate culture is not supportive and positive for the employees.

Ethics and strategic planning

Strategic planning can be defined as the process by which managers develop future courses of action for the firm to achieve its short-term and long-term goals. It is through this planning process that the ethical values of the firm are embedded into the decision-making process. Through the integration of ethics in the decision-making process, firms can identify and effectively serve the expected needs of their stakeholders. It is critical to incorporate serving stakeholders' needs into the actions of the firm since success or failure can have a significant impact on the firm's overall financial performance.

Strategic planning and the ethical cycle

It is imperative that firms incorporate the ethical needs and demands of the stakeholders into the development of their strategic plans. A framework which embraces this integration is the ethical cycle, which has six components: moral problem statement, problem analysis, options for actions, ethical judgment, reflection, and morally acceptable action.

Moral problem statement

The moral problem statement is based on the decision maker being able to identify a moral problem. When the individual perceives a moral problem, there are certain conditions which must be met before moving on to the problem analysis stage in the ethical cycle. The first condition is that there must be a clear understanding of what the moral problem is. The second condition is that there needs to be an identification of which stakeholder(s) are affected by the resolution of the moral problem. The third condition is the identification of the factual basis of the moral issue which the decision maker must resolve.

Problem analysis

To effectively analyze the moral problem, the individual must be able to identify three factors: 1) Which stakeholders currently and in the future will be impacted by the decision of the individual? 2) What is the composition of the moral values that are needed to understand and analyze the problem? 3) What are the relevant facts and information that are related to the moral problem which can be used to determine the correct course of action?

Options for action

Once the moral problem has been identified and the collection and analysis of the information has been made, the decision maker can move to the next step in the process, which is to generate viable alternative options to resolve the problem. These alternative options allow the decision maker to clarify how each option can impact the firm's stakeholders in both a positive and negative way. It is at this step in the ethical cycle that creativity and innovativeness may be necessary to force the decision maker to consider alternatives outside the individual's typical "comfort zone."

It is human nature to use heuristics in the decision-making process, which allow relatively quick decisions based on past personal experiences. Heuristics are mental shortcuts people use to quicken the decision-making process. People rely on the results of past experiences to help make current decisions. The use of heuristics is not the most effective method to be used at this stage of the ethical cycle. The convenience of using heuristics results in not looking at the full spectrum of options available to the decision maker. By making it "easier" to determine only one or two courses of action, the decision maker ignores potentially many more viable alternatives that would result in a more effective resolution of the moral problem.

Ethical judgment

Ethical judgment is based on the evaluation of the different options available to resolve the ethical issue. Each of the alternatives presented in the options for action stage of the ethical cycle are evaluated to determine which course of action would provide the maximum benefits for the maximum number of stakeholders of the firm. Ethical judgment is critical since it determines the eventual course of action for the firm.

Reflection

Reflection occurs based on the determination of the final course of action by the firm. During the reflection stage of the ethical cycle, the outcomes from the ethical judgment stage are further evaluated to determine the final, approved course of action by the decision maker. It is during the reflection stage that the ethical judgment options are weighed against each other to determine what would be considered the optimal solution to the moral problem.

Morally acceptable action

The morally acceptable action is based on the implementation of the optimal solution determined in the reflection stage. To be considered an optimal course of action, the optimal solution must be perceived to be the optimal course of action by the firm's stakeholders. A positive perception is critical since the consequences of the actions of the firm will be evaluated based on the level of integrity, transparency, and moral values by the firm's stakeholders.

Vale mining and the ethical cycle

On January 25, 2019, Dam 1 of Vale's Corrego do Feijao iron-ore mine in Brazil collapsed and killed 270 people within minutes. Over 11 million cubic meters of mining waste was released from the collapsed dam and moved at speeds of up to 50 miles an hour downhill toward the city of Brumadinho.

The dam was unsafe, and the management of Vale refused to take preventive measures to ensure the safety of the workers and residents in the local community. It was determined that there were several causes of the dam's collapse. Those causes included the use of cheap materials in the construction of the dam, Vale's managers refusing to respond to warnings about the structural problems of the dam, and the failure of the monitoring equipment.

Moral problem statement

From an ethical cycle perspective, Vale's managers failed in the first step in the process. Vale's managers refused to acknowledge that its dam was structurally unsound and would cause catastrophic damage if the dam failed. Therefore, the managers failed in the first condition of having a clear understanding of the moral problem. Vale's managers also failed in the second condition by ignoring who the critical stakeholders were and the negative consequences those stakeholders would have to endure if the dam failed. Vale's managers even failed the third condition by not seeking more information pertaining to the dangers of the dam and ignoring or discounting information that did warn them of the safety issues related to the dam.

Problem analysis

Vale's managers also did not do an effective job of analyzing the moral problem. As was stated in the previous section, Vale's managers failed to identify the potential consequences of their decisions related to its stakeholders. In addition, they downplayed the warning signs that they were given pertaining to the lack of safety of the dam.

A critical component for Vale's managers to consider was the inherent danger in the type of dam that collapsed. The dam that collapsed was a tailings dam. Tailings are the rocks and other material that are left over after the mining of the iron ore process take place. As a result, tailings could be considered the natural waste by-product of the mining process. A wall of the tailings dam is composed of tailings instead of strong materials such as concrete, metal, or wood. The tailings are dried and then used to form the dam wall. As the dam water rises, Vale would add more tailings to increase the height of the dam. Tailings dams can be easily compromised by having additional water seep into the dam, which weakens the foundation of the mine. Without controlling the water flow into a tailing dam, the dam's integrity will eventually be compromised.

In addition, the dam which collapsed was an upstream dam. An upstream dam is built on a side of a mountain above towns that are located at the base of the mountain. Upstream dams are very common in mountainous countries in South America because of their proximity to the mining operations. Being an upstream dam also creates huge safety issues since once the dam breaks, the mining waste is released and picks up speed as it moves downhill toward the local towns at the base of the mountain.

Options for action

Options for action refer to the manager's ability to develop different scenarios to address the moral issue. The use of these alternatives allows the managers to realize and understand the potential impact the decision has on the firm's stakeholders. While managers are expected to be creative and innovative in the development of multiple alternative courses of action, this was not the case for the managers at Vale. In fact, Vale relied on an external consultant, TUV SUD, to develop what the correct course of action would be related to any issues at the dam. TUV SUD filled the dual role of safety inspectors and consultants for Vale. Since TUV SUD is paid by Vale to perform safety inspections as well as providing consulting advice, there is an inherent conflict of interest. If TUV SUD wanted to have Vale as a long-term client, it would be expected that TUV SUD would tell Vale what they wanted to hear, including validating the safety of the dam.

TUV SUD had warned Vale in September 2018 that faulty water drainage and inoperative monitoring systems had increased the potential risk that the dam would collapse. The report also stated that problems with the monitoring equipment made it difficult to fully evaluate the stability of the dam. TUV SUD had also recommended that additional monitoring equipment should be included on the dam site, including a seismic monitor to be able to measure the ground activity around the dam. Despite these warnings, TUV SUD signed off that the dam was considered stable and would not collapse.

Ethical judgment

Vale did not want to focus on any different options pertaining to the safety of the dam. Without alternative scenarios, the status quo was the only option offered and the only option implemented. By only considering the status quo as a course of action, Vale's managers completely ignored a course of action which would provide the maximum benefits to the maximum number of stakeholders of the firm.

Reflection

As was stated in the previous section, the final course of action had already been predetermined by Vale's managers. The current course of action continued as the final course of action. Despite mounting evidence to show that the dam would break, Vale's managers continued to ignore any information that did not support the status quo. To justify implementing the same course of action, Vale needed and received validation that this course of action was appropriate and acceptable when TUV SUD, as the safety inspector, certified that the dam was safe. After the dam collapse, a spokeswoman of Vale stated that "Vale is committed to the safety of its structures and has a structured system to manage the dams that includes several technical and governance actions."

Morally acceptable action

Vale's managers did not implement a morally acceptable action by following the status quo. The status quo was not the optimal course of action nor was this course of action supported by the evidence of the potential dam failure. The validation that Vale's managers did not implement a morally acceptable action occurred when Brazilian police arrested eight employees on suspicion of first-degree murder in February 2019.

The following month, Vale's CEO, Fabio Schvartsman and other top Vale executives agreed to step down from their management positions based on the commencement of an investigation into whether there was criminal negligence as part of the dam collapse. In January 2020, Fabio Schvartsman and ten other Vale employees and five TUV SUD employees were charged with homicide. The prosecutors alleged that Vale and TUV SUD had systematically and intentionally hidden incriminating internally generated information about the safety issues related to tailing dams for years. One of the prosecutors in the case stated that "Vale, with the support of TUV SUD, produced a large amount of technical information about… various dams owned and managed by Vale, that were recognized… as dams with an unacceptable risk profile."

Emergent strategies and ethics

The strategic planning process assumes that the managers developing the planning can anticipate future changes that occur once the strategic plan has been implemented. This intended strategy focuses on an assumed course of action that, if effectively implemented, will result in the firm being able to achieve its goals. However, as is demonstrated with the COVID-19 crisis, the firm's intended strategies may never fully be realized.

Therefore, there will be parts of the intended strategy that are not realized. These actions are abandoned by the firm because they are no longer relevant to the implementation of the strategic plan. Portions of the strategic plan can be unrealized due to factors such as lack of resources and shifts in external factors. As the strategy moves along the implementation stage, the intended strategy becomes the deliberate strategy of the firm. The firm's deliberate strategy reflects the firm's movement toward its completed realized strategy. However, parts of the realized strategy are also factors related to an emergent strategy.

An emergent strategy is based on developing additional actions related to the firm's strategic plan which were not considered when the managers developed the intended strategy. During the implementation process, conditions can change which result in emerging factors that the firm can capitalize on to increase its performance. For example, during the COVID-19 crisis, local and federal governments ordered the closure of dining room service in restaurants to reduce the probability of spreading the virus. As a result, restaurants which never had curb side or delivery services were forced to adapt their strategic planning to include these actions for the financial survival of the restaurants. The coronavirus pandemic has resulted in every firm and organization globally identifying and adopting emergent strategies to enhance long-term survival viability. LVMH is an example of a firm which has embraced utilitarianism as part of its emergent strategy during the coronavirus pandemic.

LVMH converts perfume manufacturing to hand sanitizer

The foundation of the strategic planning process is the ability to achieve both short-term and long-term goals for the firm. However, this strategic planning process can change due to an extraordinary series of events.

As the world continues its battle to contain and then control the outbreak of COVID-19, firms have had to make quick and abrupt changes in their strategic planning. As a result, numerous emergent strategies took place in which the firms were not able to predict the shifts in market changes daily. The coronavirus also gave firms the opportunity to shift strategic planning into a more utilitarian perspective. An example of this shift occurred for the luxury goods manufacturer, LVMH. LVMH owns brands such as Louis Vuitton, Christian Dior, Fendi, Givenchy, Tag Heuer, and Hennessy.

On March 20, 2020, LVMH announced that it was going to convert three of its perfume manufacturing facilities, which usually make fragrances for Christian Dior, Givenchy, and Guerlain, into manufacturing hand sanitizer. LVMH estimated that it would be able to produce 12 tons of hand sanitizer (hydroalcoholic gel) weekly. LVMH did not sell the gel but gave it to French authorities and hospitals in Europe for free.

This altruistic action by LVMH addresses the needs of all its stakeholders because, regardless of which vested interest the individual has with LVMH operations, all its stakeholders are humans who are threatened by the coronavirus. It gives the firm a strong positive image and enhances its reputation to its stakeholders. In addition, keeping those manufacturing facilities open results in continued employment for its employees despite LVMH absorbing 100 percent of the costs of production.

LVMH also broadened the definition of a luxury good. The traditional perspective of a luxury good is a high-quality, high price-exclusive product. LVMH has adjusted that definition to define a true luxury business as one that will meet the needs of its customers at the highest level, which includes access to hand sanitizer during a pandemic. In the re-enforcement of its commitment to the safety of the community instead of its own self-interests, LVMH has not put a "brand" name on the hand sanitizer. LVMH is not seeking this action as a marketing opportunity but as an opportunity to use its resources for the betterment of others.

Ethical strategic planning in a crisis

An ethical crisis can occur when an event occurs which is not part of the firm's normal course of action. From pandemic to product recalls, firms must be able to effectively respond to these crises in an ethical manner. Firms need to be able to develop and implement a disaster plan that has been created before the crisis starts so that the firm can follow an optimal course of action. An ethical crisis can be classified as internal-normal, internal-abnormal, external-normal, and external-abnormal.

Internal-normal

An ethical crisis that is internal and normal occurs within the firm and the situation of the crisis can be predictable. Due to its high level of predictability, the firm has the opportunity to develop an emergency pre-crisis plan before the event occurs. Examples of these types of crises include product failures or recalls, allegations of sexual harassment, workplace violence, vandalism, or an employee strike.

Internal-abnormal

A crisis that is internal and abnormal also occurs within the firm, but the crisis is usually rare and unpredictable. Since it is rare and unpredictable, it is more difficult for the firm to have already developed an emergency pre-crisis plan that can be used during the crisis. Examples of these types of crises include corporate scandals, hacking and other forms of information theft, copyright infringement, and falsification of information.

External-normal

A crisis that is external and normal is predictable in nature and occurs outside the firm. Since the crisis is external in nature, there could be multiple firms which also must address the same crisis. Examples of these types of crises include global shortages of raw materials, supplier failures, industrial espionage, failure in complete categories of products, and technology attacks that are industry wide.

External-abnormal

A crisis that is external and abnormal is rare and is based on events that are external to the firm. The crisis is virtually impossible to predict, and the consequences of the crisis are also difficult to determine. The coronavirus pandemic is an example of this type of crisis. Other examples include acts of terrorism, natural disasters, and attacks on a firm's reputation.

While an internal and normal crisis is considered to be the most common type of crisis, the act of selling a potentially fatal product can be devastating. When human lives are at risk, the crisis moves beyond a simple product failure or recall. An example of the dangers of selling a product that can permanently alter the lives of people and their family members is the thalidomide story.

Thalidomide: The wonder drug that wasn't

In early 1960, an expecting mother in Toronto, Canada was prescribed a drug by her physician to help with her morning sickness. The drug was developed in Germany to relieve symptoms including anxiety, headaches, and morning sickness, and was described as being safer than Alka-Seltzer. The drug, thalidomide, was not a miracle drug but caused devastating birth defects including shortened arms and missing fingers. Even more severe birth defects included babies not having any arms or legs while other babies had no ears or malformed kidneys.

Thalidomide was developed by a former Nazi war criminal, Dr. Heinrich Muckter, for the German pharmaceutical company, Chemie Grunenthal. The drug was sold throughout Germany without any trials. The drug was prescribed to pregnant women and was marketed as a safe alternative to sedatives, which could lead to overdoses. Grunenthal expanded the market of thalidomide to other countries and expanded the claims of its benefits for multiple ailments, including morning sickness and relieving anxiety. It is estimated that approximately 10,000 babies born primarily in Germany, Britain, and Australia were born with these defects in the 1950s and 1960s. The resulting defects were a consequence of the mothers taking the drug.

In 1956 and 1957, the American pharmaceutical firm Smith, Kline & French distributed the drug to numerous doctors through a clinical trial. The drug had not been approved by the Federal Drug Administration (FDA) so Smith, Kline & French could not legally sell the drug. During the clinical trial, the doctors were not told the drug was thalidomide, but instead were given the code name of SK&F #5627. It is assumed this was done since the doctors in the United States may have heard of thalidomide and the devastating side effects and would have refused to give it to their patients. Smith, Kline & French concluded the drug did not support the claims from Grunenthal and did not apply for the drug to be sold in the United States.

However, another American pharmaceutical firm, Richardson-Merrell, was selling thalidomide in Canada under the brand name of Kevadon and was aggressively pursuing approval to sell the drug in the United States. As part of Richardson-Merrell's marketing of thalidomide to American doctors, the firm assured the doctors that they did not need to keep track of which patients took the drug. In fact, the salesmen were told to tell the doctors that they did not need to "…sacrifice having an important man evaluate Kevadon for the sake of case histories." It is again assumed that Richardson-Merrell recommended not keeping track of the drug because that data could be submitted as evidence in any future lawsuit against the firm.

To add to the confusion, Richardson-Merrell had manufactured thalidomide in a variety of different shapes and colors. Despite its best efforts, Richardson-Merrell never received approval to sell the drug in the United States because one FDA reviewer, Dr. Frances Kelsey, was concerned about the safety of the drug and delayed the approval of the application.

In November 1961, Grunenthal withdrew thalidomide from the German market due to the concerns related to birth defects and Richardson-Merrell later followed by withdrawing its application for approval. In the fall of 1962, the FDA determined that Richardson-Merrell had violated the law by selling the drug without FDA approval multiple times. It was also alleged that company lawyers had destroyed incriminating internal memos related to management's discussion of thalidomide. The drug was given to approximately 20,000 Americans, including pregnant women. Since detailed records were not made of who was given the drug, there is no confirmed estimate of how many babies in the United States had birth defects related to thalidomide.

The dangerous side effects of thalidomide resulted in the United States implementing strict drug safety laws requiring pharmaceutical companies to prove their drugs had been evaluated based on rigorous clinical trials. This story from over 60 years ago is still important today in ensuring that all drugs that are given to patients have been through numerous rigorous trials to ensure the short-term and long-term safety of the patient.

The woman at the beginning of this story was Peter's mother, Olive Stanwick. When she was prescribed thalidomide by her doctor, even though she did not know the dangers of the drug, she said "No thank you, I would rather have morning sickness than risk the health of my baby by taking a drug I don't need." Peter is forever grateful for that decision.

Ethics and corporate culture

Corporate culture can be defined as the shared values and beliefs of the employees within a firm. It is imperative that a firm has a strong corporate culture to support and champion the strong ethical values of the employees. The manifestation of culture is represented within the firm based on factors such as artifacts, rituals, and traditions. Artifacts can be physical representations of the firm's culture including the dress code of the firm, what type of cafeteria is available to the employees, whether managers are allowed to fly first class, and the physical design of the workplace. Rituals and traditions that could be based on employees using storytelling to transfer information about the firm's culture to other employees. Traditions could also be something as simple as company events such as annual company picnics and annual sales conferences in which the best-performing sales representatives are recognized and rewarded.

One of the operational benefits of having a strong positive culture is that it can be used to establish structural stability and facilitate the integration of different operational components within the firm. Firms can improve overall operations by capitalizing on the benefits of having a strong positive culture. There are two major components of a strong culture: employees having a high level of agreement about ethical values and employees having a high motivation to support and protect those values in how they interact with the firm's stakeholders.

Components of an ethical culture

There are several components of a strong ethical culture:

1. There are a clear set of organizational values that emphasize the firm's commitment to corporate compliance, integrity, and business ethics.
2. The executive leadership sets the tone in their actions by leading by example. The executive leadership not only guides the ethical commitment of the employees, but they also provide the benchmark for what is acceptable and unacceptable behavior.
3. The top-level executives must also be consistent with their messaging to the stakeholders. The messaging must be transparent and concise.
4. The managers below the top-level managers, who are the front-line and mid-level supervisors, must ensure that the ethical commitment of the firm is incorporated within the actions of the employees. It is these middle-level managers who can use cultural tools such as stories and traditions to reinforce the ethical values of the firm.

5. The firm must establish a corporate climate which allows the employees to be comfortable in asking questions and raising concerns about ethical issues without being concerned about retaliation. The firm must establish an anonymous communication system to allow the employees to be a "whistleblower" and inform the firm of potential unethical behavior.

6. The top-level executives need explicit accountability in their actions to expect the same level of accountability to lower-level managers and employees.

7. The underlying philosophy of the hiring process is the expectation that the employees the firm hires will want to stay employed by the firm. This "hire to retire" life cycle strengthens the ethical fabric of the firm by creating loyalty for employees who have both strong character and a high level of competence.

8. The firm must have a strong incentives and reward system to ensure the employees are rewarded both intrinsically and extrinsically. Positive examples of strong ethical behavior should not only be rewarded but should be shown in the same light as rituals and traditions since this behavior can be replicated by other employees in the future if the need arises.

Nehemiah Manufacturing: Where ethical values are part of Nehemiah's cultural DNA

At Nehemiah Manufacturing, the cultural artifacts are not based on having yoga classes and free lunches in the cafeteria. Employee perks include social-service support and an attorney. In 2010, the founders of Nehemiah decided to create a firm which would give job opportunities to people in a lower income section of Cincinnati. The result was that Nehemiah started hiring people who had a criminal background and were given a second chance. By 2020, approximately 80 percent of the firm's 180 employees have a criminal background. Nehemiah manufactures various consumer products such as Boogie Wipes and Saline Soothers.

The president of Nehemiah, Richard Palmer, stated that "We are investing in our employees in order to retain them… It's no different than tech companies bringing in lunch and a foosball table." The initial hiring started in 2011 with several significant challenges Nehemiah had to address with its employees including substance abuse, mental illness, and being homeless. Nehemiah hired a social-service worker that was able to help employees address issues ranging from finding housing to keeping the employees off drugs and alcohol.

Nehemiah currently has a three-person social-services team which facilitates the holistic development of the employees. For example, Nehemiah not only helps employees to find housing but also helps them improve their credit record and teaches them how to develop and maintain a personal budget. The stability of these jobs allowed the employees to rebuild personal relationships with family and friends.

Richard Palmer noticed that employees with a criminal background are extremely appreciative of the opportunity to have a job and they show that appreciation by having a fierce level of loyalty to Nehemiah. Palmer commented about the employees' loyalty by stating that "When we were looking for people to work overtime, come in on Saturday or go that extra mile, it was the second-chance population that was saying, 'I'm in'."

Nehemiah spends approximately $120,000 annually on its social-service team and donates $150,000 a year to different non-profit organizations including City Gospel Mission. City Gospel Mission sends job candidates to Nehemiah and is able to offer drug treatment and rehab programs to Nehemiah's employees. Nehemiah also has an attorney who helps employees address issues such as trying to get their criminal records expunged and providing advice if the employee needs to go into bankruptcy to start anew financially. Nehemiah also provides $50,000 for continuing education and rents out the four apartments it owns to employees at half the market rates.

Dan Meyer, Nehemiah's CEO, explains the rationale of providing all these services to its employees. "Can I cut some of this stuff and make a little more money? I sure don't want to… This is a business model about a social enterprise making money."

Ethics and corporate compliance

Corporate compliance refers to the evaluation of how a firm conforms to laws and regulations through its policies and procedures. The firm is responsible for establishing a formal process for its global operations to ensure it is not in violation with the current laws in the countries in which it operates. It is part of the compliance process to minimize the financial and non-financial risk of non-compliance.

The distinction between ethics and compliance refers to the firm complying with all laws and regulations, which moves ethics up a level to includes incorporating ethical values in the decision-making process of the firm's managers. Therefore, a firm can be compliant without being ethical. From the corporate social responsibility pyramid perspective, compliance is meeting the legal stage of the pyramid while ethics moves one step higher and embraces the ethical stage of the pyramid. Therefore, compliance is meeting the legal standard of doing the right thing while ethics is meeting the standard of doing the right thing even if it is not the most profitable action to take.

Swedbank and the lack of corporate compliance

As one of the largest banks in Sweden, Swedbank has a strong commitment to corporate compliance. In the compliance section of its website, it states that the board of directors has the overall responsibility for its operations and the CEO is responsible for establishing formal procedures to ensure compliance with all laws and regulations. Swedbank also claims that its compliance work will help, maintain, and reinforce Swedbank's reputation and trustworthiness. Its actions also include efforts to "…strive to reduce the risk of legal sanctions or loss of reputation due to inadequate adherence to regulations."

From this bravado narrative, it was surprising to see that on March 19, 2020, Swedbank was fined $397 million for failing to comply with anti-money laundering regulations. The Swedish financial supervisory authority had determined that Swedbank had serious deficiencies in its anti-money laundering measures in its Estonian branch. The investigation started when a Swedish broadcaster had reported the suspicious activity in 2019. The Swedish authority also disclosed that Swedbank was aware of the Estonian branch's lack of proper processes, routines, and control systems to ensure the branch was not participating in money laundering.

Swedbank had been given several internal and external reports pertaining to the money laundering and failed to take proper and corrective action. Swedbank was also accused of withholding documentation and information related to money laundering during the investigation. In response to the fine, Swedbank's CEO, Jens Henriksson, admitted that "Swedbank has failed to uphold the trust of customers, owners and society… This is troublesome and very serious."

Of course, having the CEO admit that these allegations are very serious and troublesome does not soothe the anger of Swedbank's stakeholders who assumed that the firm had followed the proper procedures to ensure full compliance. It is especially concerning to the shareholders of the firm since money laundering is always a paramount issue in any financial institution. While this crisis may be perceived as internal and normal, there should not be any rationale in which this type of criminal activity can occur unchecked within a major financial institution.

Bibliography

Berardino, Mike. 2012. Mike Tyson Explains One of His Most Famous Quotes. *South Florida Sun Sentinel*. November 9.

Chopping, Dominic. 2020. Swedbank Fined $397 Million Over Anti-Money Laundering Measures. *The Wall Street Journal*. March 19.

Kestenbaum, Richard. 2020. LVMH Converting Its Perfume Factories to Make Hand Sanitizer. *Forbes*. March 15.

Mintzberg, Henry and James A. Waters. 1985. Of Strategies, Deliberate and Emergent. *Strategic Management Journal*. 6:3. 257–272.

Nogueira, Marta. 2020. Brazil Charges Ex-Vale CEO with Homicide for Dam Disaster. *Reuters*. January 21.

Sandford, Nicole. 2015. Corporate Culture: The Center of Strong Ethics and Compliance. *The Wall Street Journal*. January 20.

Simon, Ruth. 2020. The Company of Second Chances. *The Wall Street Journal*. January 25.

Stanwick, Peter and Sarah Stanwick. 2019. The Vale Brazilian Dam Collapse: An Ethical and Engineering Disaster. *American Journal of Sciences and Engineering Research*. 2(6). 6–11.

Swedbank website. www.swedbank.com/about-swedbank/management-and-corporate-governance/internal-control-and-auditing/compliance.html

Thomas, Katie. 2020. The Unseen Survivors of Thalidomide Want to Be Heard. *The New York Times*. March 23.

van de Poel, Ibo and Lambèr Royakkers. 2007. The Ethical Cycle. *Journal of Business Ethics*. 71:1. 1–13.

Weinstein, Bruce. 2020. What's the Difference Between Compliance and Ethics. *Forbes*. May 9.

5   Decision-making and human resource issues

Essential summary

An individual's moral compass is that intuition which individuals rely on to determine right from wrong. The foundation use of each person's moral compass is in his/her decisions and how the person treats fellow employees. For the compass to continue to point due north, it is the responsibility of the individual to mature not only physically and emotionally, but also morally. The chapter starts with the seminal work of Kohlberg in the identification of his six states of moral development. The evolution of the maturity of individuals based on their moral beliefs is paramount in determining how and why individuals make decisions related to ethical issues. An ethical dilemma about a man and his dying wife called the Heinz dilemma applies Kohlberg's six stages of moral development to highlight the difficult task in determining the appropriate course of action.

The chapter continues with another seminal work, the study done by Stanley Milgram, which determines to what lengths individuals will go to please an authority figure. While "just following orders" was not an acceptable defense in the Nuremberg trials for Nazi criminals, Milgram concluded that orders given by superiors is a powerful influencer in the decisions made by subordinates, regardless of the circumstances.

Milgram's study of obedience is followed by the role of power and influence and how these constructs are critical to the success of any manager. However, there can be the temptation to abuse power to the detriment of those impacted by these decisions. This abuse of power is explicitly presented in the discussion of Machiavellianism and the importance of manipulation in order to obtain the individual's desired goals.

The chapter continues with a discussion of ethical issues related to human resources. The potential unethical and illegal activities related to the hiring process including implicit and explicit biases demonstrate that every manager must be transparent to themselves on the selection and hiring process of job candidates.

Kohlberg's six stages of moral development

One of the fundamental concepts of ethical decision making is the ability of an individual to evolve through moral development. The underlying premise of moral development is that just as an individual physically and emotionally matures, so does the individual's level of moral development. Lawrence Kohlberg presents a six-stage process in which moral development of the individual evolves. The stages are separated into three levels which are Preconventional: Stage 1 obedience and punishment orientation and Stage 2 instrumental purpose and exchange; Conventional: Stage 3 interpersonal accord, conformity, and mutual expectations and Stage 4 social accord and system maintenance; and Post-Conventional: Stage 5 social contract and individual rights and Stage 6 universal ethical principles.

Preconventional stages

Stage 1: Obedience and punishment orientation (obedience)

Stage 1 is based on the basic human instincts of behavior modification due to consequences and repercussions of the individual's actions. The individual's moral decisions are shaped based on the reaction of others to the individual's behavior. This behavior modification is a common tool used by parents in modifying the behavior of children by highlighting to them what is right and wrong. Based on being punished for unacceptable behavior, the child will change his/her behavior to ensure the child will not be punished in the future.

Stage 2: Instrumental purpose and exchange (self-interest)

The evolution of the moral values of individuals starts at Stage 2 where individuals interpret the rules regarding their behavior and then integrate those rules into their own behavior. It is at this stage that the individual determines whether the rules serve their self-interests, and if they do, the rules will be followed. It is through this transactional process that the individual links the benefits of his/her actions with the potential costs and consequences.

Conventional stages

Stage 3: Interpersonal accord, conformity, and mutual expectations (conformity)

In Stage 3, individuals behave according to what is expected of them or by others. It is through mutual respect and interpersonal relations that the individual conforms to the expectations of society. It is the expectations from society that determine the behavior of the individual. The development of the individual's social conscience is integrated in the decision-making process to determine what is right or wrong. There is an expectation that if the individual behaves in a manner that is in agreement with the values of society, the individual will also be treated by individuals in the same manner based on the societal framework of moral behavior.

Stage 4: Social accord and system maintenance (maintaining society)

In Stage 4, decisions are made by the individual based on the obligations and duties that have been acknowledged and accepted by them. The evolution of moral development takes place by the individual understanding that a commitment needs to be made to uphold the law and improve society. The exception to this commitment is if the individual perceives that a different course of action in needed for society in the future. The underlying philosophy of Stage 4 is that everyone has to fulfill their obligation to society since a lack of obligation can result in a society in chaos.

Post-conventional morality stages

Stage 5: Social contract and individual rights (utilitarian-based laws)

At Stage 5, moral development evolves to understand the utilitarian value of laws. Individuals separate themselves from their own self-interests and view society through the cognitive lens that supports laws and actions that benefit the greatest number in society. The individual understands and supports the rules that agree with society's social contract. It is through these perceived social contracts that individuals have an agreement with the government pertaining to the guidelines of moral behavior.

Stage 6: Universal ethical principles

Stage 6 is the pinnacle of moral development for the individual. Individuals can govern their actions based on their chosen ethical principles. The principles are perceived to be universal in scope, which gives individuals their own justification to violate laws that do not coincide with their principles. Apartheid laws in South Africa and segregation laws in the United States would be examples concerning whether the universal ethical principle of human rights supersedes the laws established by the government. Therefore, what is right drives the decision-making process and violating laws can demonstrate to the government why those laws are not the correct course of action for society.

Heinz dilemma

The Heinz dilemma is an ethical dilemma which can facilitate the determination of which stage an individual is at based on Kohlberg's stages of moral development. The individual is given the following scenario.

> *A woman is dying from a special type of cancer and there is only one drug which could potentially save her from death. The derivate of the drug is the radioactive material radium. A local druggist had discovered the drug and was asking ten times the price of the drug to sell to customers. The druggist had paid $200 for the radium and charged $2,000 for a small dose of the drug. Heinz, the husband of the dying woman, could not afford to pay the $2,000 and asked all his friends for money. He was only able to obtain $1,000 to pay for the drug. He went to the druggist and asked whether he would take $1,000 for the drug or take $1,000 now and he would pay him the rest at a later time. The druggist refused by claiming that since he had discovered the drug, he had the right to set the price of the drug. Heinz broke into the drug store and stole the drug for his wife.*

In order to evaluate the individual's stage of moral development, the question to ask is whether or not Heinz should steal the drug.

Preconventional stages

Stage 1: Obedience

If the individual is at Stage 1, the decision would be to not steal the drug because stealing is breaking the law and Heinz will be punished. This is the simplest explanation for the decision because it converted the ethical decision into a legal decision. This decision rejects any special circumstances where it is considered to be "appropriate" to break the law.

Stage 2: Self-interest

By Stage 2, the framework has changed to how to resolve the ethical dilemma. Self-interest can be a justification for either stealing the drug or not stealing the drug. If Heinz steals the drug, he potentially saves the life of his wife. Therefore, it is in his own self-interest to steal the drug. However, it is also in his own self-interest if he does not steal the drug. If he does not steal the drug, he avoids being arrested and sent to prison.

Conventional stages

Stage 3: Conformity

At Stage 3, the focus shifts to how Heinz perceives his actions will be interpreted by others. At the conformity stage, Heinz could justify stealing the drug since he is expected by society to help his wife regardless of the risk. Therefore, stealing the drug would confirm his belief that others would react in the same situation. The analogy is "walk a mile in my shoes," which refers to Heinz asking others to see his actions as if they were in the same situation. Alternatively, Heinz could also argue that not stealing the drug is consistent with conformity with society. Since stealing is illegal, Heinz will conform to societal expectations if he respects the law and does not steal the drug but continues to seek alternative methods in order to obtain the drug.

Stage 4: Maintaining society

At Stage 4, Heinz shifts his focus to considering his actions based on trying to maintain a society in which individuals respect the laws of the land. It is through this perspective that Heinz could argue that he should not steal the drug since if this was the decision of everyone there would be no respect for law and order. Society will turn into a chaotic climate in which everyone will only focus on their own needs. However, Heinz could also argue that stealing the drug would also support the rules of society by agreeing that his actions are wrong and that it is society's role to punish him for his behavior.

Post-conventional stages

Stage 5: Social contracts–utilitarian based laws

At Stage 5, the shift for Heinz is based on the philosophical belief that his actions are based on a social contract he has with society. From a social contract perspective, Heinz could argue that it is acceptable to steal the drug since it is inferred that people have the right to do whatever means necessary in order not to die. Therefore, if society supports a climate in which human survival is desirable, stealing the drug to potentially save his wife from dying is justified. However, it can also be argued that the druggist's actions should also be rewarded within a social contract framework. The basis of a capitalistic system is to receive financial rewards for inventions by being able to capitalize on one's own ideas. In addition, the druggist would argue that it is within his social contract to be able to set the price of a drug based on his innovation. Therefore, the druggist should receive full compensation with the payment of $2,000 in exchange for the potentially lifesaving drug.

Stage 6: Universal ethical principles

As was mentioned in the previous section, Stage 6 is the pinnacle of moral development. It is at this stage that the individual embraces ethical principles that are universal in scope. At Stage 6, Heinz would argue that individuals have a universal right to live and have the right to do whatever is necessary in order to stay alive. This human right is the basis of the survival of the human race. Heinz would argue that he had to steal the drug in order to give his wife the right to survival and this rationale is consistent globally. Alternatively, Heinz could also argue that everyone in the world has the same human right to survival and there may be other people with the same type of cancer but who would have a better chance of recovery by taking the drug than his wife.

Obedience and the decision-making process

In 1963, a psychologist from Yale University, Stanley Milgram, wanted to answer a very simple question: Would people willingly break their own moral and ethical values because they were told to by a person of authority? The origin of the study was based on the Nuremberg trials at the end of World War II. During those trials, German Nazi soldiers claimed that they had no choice in the actions of killing millions of people because they had to follow orders from their commanders. If they did not follow orders they would be demoted or killed. The defense of following orders was not considered a valid reason for killing innocent people at the Nuremberg trials. Milgram wanted to determine whether that same type of obedience could occur in a non-wartime setting using randomly selected individuals from New Haven, Connecticut where Yale University is located.

Milgram's study included 40 men between the ages of 20 and 50 who had been selected based on responding to an advertisement for the study. The study was described in the advertisement as one in which the volunteers would test the memory and learning capabilities of subjects at Yale University. The occupations of the volunteers included salesmen, engineers, manual laborers, postal workers, and high school students. The description of the study based on testing the memory of the subjects was to ensure that the volunteers did not know the true focus of the study, which was to determine to what extent the volunteers would follow orders even if the result may cause death.

The volunteers were sent into a room which had a fake electric shock generator machine. A man in a white lab coat gave the volunteers instructions about the study. The volunteers asked the subjects a series of questions and if the subjects gave the wrong answer, they were shocked. The machine did not give out any shocks and the subjects were working with Milgram in order to pretend they were receiving the shocks. For each wrong answer, the volunteer would increase the voltage of the "shocks." The range of shock on the machine was from 15 to 450 volts. At the highest shock level, there was a warning sign which stated "Danger: Severe Shock." The volunteers were able to hear the subjects crying out to stop due to pain as the shock level increased.

As the "shocks" increased, so did the level of "screaming" of the subjects. When the volunteer became hesitant to move to the next set of questions, the man in the lab coat told the volunteer to continue with the testing since it was important that the volunteer complete the test. When the shock reached the high range, the subject would pretend to become unconscious and the volunteer would continue to give shocks even when there was not a response from the subject. While Milgram had thought that only a small number of volunteers would obey the order to give a potentially deadly shock of 450 volts, he was mistaken. The results showed that all 40 volunteers were willing to give a potentially dangerous shock of 240 volts and 26 of the 40 volunteers were willing to give the likely fatal shock of 450 volts. Therefore, 65 percent or almost two-thirds of volunteers were willing to give a shock which would likely kill the subject. Milgram had confirmed that human nature includes respect and obedience to authority even if it contrasts with the individual's moral and ethical values.

The role of power and influence in decision making

Power

Power is a necessary tool for all managers. A manager has to have the authority to make decisions but also have the ability to make sure the decisions are executed in an effective manner. From an ethical standpoint, it can become a gray area as to when legitimate authority ends and an abuse of power begins.

A manager must meet two standards in order to use power in an ethical manner. The first standard is that the manager's power must be exercised to benefit and serve others. This standard is based on the belief that the manager's decisions are in the beneficial interests of the firm and its stakeholders. The second standard is that the power used by the manager conforms to both the legal standard and cultural standards of what is considered to be ethical behavior.

Managers have both formal and informal power. Formal power is based on the power related to the manager's job title. For example, a manager has formal power over his/her subordinates based on a manager's supervisory position. Informal power is power that a manager can develop over time. Informal power increases as a manager builds strong positive relationships with others. Almost charismatic in nature, informal power is the result of others wanting the manager to succeed and the employees will agree to follow the directions of the manager even though the manager does not have formal authority over the individuals.

Influence

Influence is the ability to change the viewpoint of someone based on either verbal and/or nonverbal actions. Power is an attribute people have but influence is an action which anyone can do. Influence can yield the same result as using power; however, a manager does not have to exercise his/her formal power if the manager can influence people to change their behaviors. As a result, a manager can "save" the direct use of power to change the actions of another person when influence is not a viable option.

Influence is an ethical action where the individual is transparent about the motives of the influence. An individual can use influence in an ethical manner if he/she explains the rationale behind the use of the persuasion to have the other individuals change their decision-making processes. If the individual is not transparent about the attempt to influence the behavior of another person, this is manipulation and is considered unethical.

Manipulation is unethical since the true intentions of the person are opaque and may only be revealed after the altered decision has been implemented. A true expert in manipulation may be so effective that the true intentions are never fully realized by the person who was manipulated. An example of an effective method of manipulation is Machiavellianism.

Machiavellianism and ethics

With the publication of his book, *The Prince*, Niccolò Machiavelli presented a roadmap of how to use manipulation to achieve one's own goals. *The Prince* tells of the story of how a prince was able to obtain and maintain his power through manipulation. To succeed using his own self-interests, the prince (or leader) must disregard any ethical and moral values with the goal being that the end result always justifies the means to get to that result.

It is the mission of the leader to be able to eliminate any opposition by any means necessary. By destroying the current opposition, the leader sends a message that it would not be wise to challenge the leader or else you will face the same fate. The description that Machiavelli gives of the perfect leader is one who is able to manipulate others with ease, who is bold and strong with his actions and is able to hide the true intentions of his actions. The strength of his actions is reflected in one of the famous quotes from *The Prince*, which is "It is better to be feared than to be loved."

It is now possible for anyone to evaluate their level of Machiavellianism. Through a survey called Mach-IV, individuals answer a series of question to determine which level of Machiavelli is embedded in the person's personality. Some of the questions of the survey include "Do you never tell anyone the true reason you do something unless there is some benefit?" and "Is it true that everyone has a vicious streak in them and it will emerge when given an opportunity?"

Ethics and human resources

Firms can capitalize on the benefits of having a strong positive ethical workplace climate in their human resources practices. From the recruitment and selection process through to retaining valuable employees who do not leave the firm, a positive workplace climate can increase profitability through both the reduction of costs and increase in revenues. The integration of ethical values in a positive workplace climate results in the firm expecting, supporting, and rewarding employees whose actions are consistent with the overall ethical commitment of the firm.

Having a positive ethical workplace environment increases the level of employee job satisfaction since employees are being treated fairly and objectively and are motivated to enhance both their individual and firm performance. A strong ethical workplace climate reinforces the positive aspects of the employee's job and also decreases the level of ambiguity by having the ethical climate supported by establishing the ethical conduct of the employees through formalized policies and procedures.

Supporting employees' decisions and actions means that they develop and entrench their overall commitment to the firm. This commitment results in the employees not only being loyal to the firm, but also being committed to the firm achieving its short-term and long-term goals. This type of commitment can become emotional for the employee and can be viewed as the development of a psychological bond connecting the employee with the firm.

Since employee commitment is so critical to the success of the firm, it is critical that the firm is able to identify potential employees in the recruitment and selection process to ensure that once these individuals are hired as employees, they will create this emotional bond with the firm. Therefore, in addition to recruiting and selecting individuals based on their technical and interpersonal skills, a critical task of the human resources department of any firm is to ensure that these individuals match the firm's ethical commitment and vision.

Ethics and the employee hiring process

The underlying assumption pertaining to ethical values of the employees and the firm is that it is a two-way street. Just as the firm expects the employees to act in an ethical manner, employees and potential employees also expect the firm to act in an ethical manner in the hiring and evaluation process.

While the expectation is that the selection and evaluation of employees is based on objective criteria, there can be implicit and/or explicit biases which taint this process. Implicit bias occurs when a decision is made based on previous experiences which are interpreted subjectively. The decision maker is not aware that he or she is making a decision based on this bias.

One example of implicit bias is if the job candidate has similar characteristics to the recruiter. If the job candidate has similar interests and/or a similar background, then the recruiter, the decision maker, may "like" this job candidate more and want this candidate to be hired. This is a potential personal bond between them which will enhance the attractiveness of hiring the job applicant. Therefore, there will be a bias toward hiring new job candidates that are perceived as part of the same group as the decision maker and a bias toward not hiring new job candidates who are not part of the same group as the decision maker.

Explicit bias is when there is a conscious effort to create bias in the decision-making process. For example, if a hiring advertisement states that the requirements include only applicants or a certain gender, age range, or ethnic group, this would be explicit bias and be both unethical and unlawful.

Hiring practices and implicit bias

Therefore, as firms become more globalized, there is an increased necessity for firms to have a high level of diversity in its employees. By bringing in alternative perspectives based on diverse backgrounds, firms are able to more effectively address the needs of its global stakeholders. There are numerous ways that decision makers can reduce the incidence of implicit bias in the hiring process and increase the level of diversity in the decision-making process.

CHECK THE JOB DESCRIPTION

The choice of words is critical in the description of a job posting. For example, words such as dominant, aggressive, and competitive in describing the personality of the job applicant may create a bias toward men applying for the job since these traits are positively associated with men in the workplace and negatively associated with women. A description of candidates as "up and coming" or "fresh" can imply a bias toward younger applicants. Alternatively, the job description should include diversity-supporting language such as "seeking experiences from different regions."

RECRUIT OUTSIDE YOUR COMFORT ZONE

It is in the comfort zone for recruiters to seek job candidates from familiar places such as their alma mater and regions close to where they live. In order to combat this implicit bias, recruiters need to focus on the qualification requirements of the job first and then determine which universities and regions they need to focus on in order to acquire a large and diverse recruiting pool of applicants.

EVALUATE EVERY RESUME IN THE SAME MANNER

Implicit bias can occur if the resumes are not reviewed in a systematic manner. For example, researchers at Rutgers and Syracuse universities developed a study to determine if there was bias in the recruitment process. The researchers sent resumes and cover letters from ficti- tious candidates for thousands of accounting jobs. The only distinction between the resumes and cover letters were that some of the candidates had identified a disability in their correspondences with the firms. The disability described in the correspondence was either a spinal cord injury or Asperger's syndrome. The applicants were given six years or one year's work experience.

The results showed that firms were 34 percent less likely to show interest in the experienced disabled candidate and 15 percent less likely to show interest in the candidate with one year of work experience. The lack of interest meant that the firm did not correspond at all with the job applicant and, therefore, did not even attempt to understand whether the disability could have an impact on the applicant's job performance. The researchers speculated that the higher rejection rate of the more experienced candidates was due to the potential higher investment costs, including higher salaries. These results showed the potential challenges of enforcing the Americans with Disabilities Act, a federal law passed in 1990 which bans discrimination against individuals who have disabilities.

IDENTIFY WHAT THE FIRM'S NEEDS ARE BEFORE YOU START THE
INTERVIEW PROCESS

Implicit bias can occur when candidates have two different, but equal, qualifications and the candidate chosen is based on a connection with the recruiter. For example, a recruiter may favor education over experience if the recruiter connects with the educational background of one candi- date versus another candidate. The net result of this bias is that another candidate with a different educational background may have a better overall fit with the job position. The establishment of transparency about qualifications during the selection process, and communication of these objective qualifications to the job candidates, creates a fair and ethical hiring practice in the firm.

STICK TO THE SCRIPT DURING THE INTERVIEW PROCESS

It is imperative that the recruiters follow the prepared script to obtain standardized data about the job applicant. Implicit bias will have a ten- dency to emerge if the discussion moves away from the requirements of the job and toward personal interests and similar experiences. These personal discussions strengthen the in-group bias between the recruiter and the job candidate.

ENSURE THAT THE DECISIONS ARE BASED ON THE CORRECT METRICS

While traditional metrics such as the candidate's alma mater, their technical experience, and their past work experience are extremely effective in determining what candidate should be hired, there may be additional metrics which are also critical for the candidate to be successful with the job placement. The ability to start a conversation for a sales representative position or the ability to quickly adapt to changes for a military position may supersede these traditional metrics in importance.

THE ABILITY TO CONTINUALLY ANALYZE THE HIRING PROCESS

While the perception by the recruiter is that no implicit biases have occurred in the hiring process, it is imperative that the hiring decisions be reviewed in aggregate. Using business analytics, firms can determine if there are biases in the hiring patterns of the firm. If certain ethnic groups or regions are underrepresented in the selection of new employees, the firm must revisit the hiring process to determine how these hiring problems can be resolved. This is both the ethical and legal course of action which the firm must take to ensure a positive ethically supported workplace climate.

Tokyo medical university student selection process: An example of explicit bias

In 2006, the top-level executives at Tokyo Medical University had a perceived problem: they had too many women applying to medical school. This was a "problem" since the underlying assumption was that women leave the workforce at a higher rate than men in order to take care of their children and families. The executives "solved" this problem by programming the computer which scores the university's entrance exam to deduct points from the score if a woman had taken the entrance exam. In 2018, the ratio of the entering class to medical school was four men to every woman. The rigging of the admission process was discovered as part of a larger investigation of Tokyo Medical University, which was also under suspicion of taking bribes from Japanese families in order to have their child attend medical school.

In contrast to the previous section which describes how to reduce or eliminate bias in the hiring process, Tokyo Medical University also applied explicit bias in the interview process for medical school candidates. The interviewers would ask the women if they are planning on getting married and having children and then would ask how they could take care of their family responsibilities as well as their responsibilities at work. In 2016, only 21 percent of doctors in Japan were women, which ranked lowest among the 36 countries which are part of the Organization for Economic Cooperation and Development.

Managers and toxic workplace climate

Managers who do not properly assume their responsibilities can become not only ineffective but may also have a negative influence on the workplace climate. This "toxic"-like atmosphere can result in significant dysfunction and can lead to an overall poor performance of the work unit. In this type of toxic culture, innovation is not encouraged, employees do not trust each other, potential bullying of employees can occur, and the manager may focus more on the accumulation of power instead of the dispersion of power.

In addition, this type of dysfunction can result in a lack of employee loyalty, which results in a high level of employee turnover. The best-performing employees will leave a toxic culture since they will have many opportunities to move to firms with more positive and supportive cultures for the employees.

There are numerous examples of how a toxic culture driven by a toxic manager can result in an unproductive workplace.

Employees are not able to make decisions

In a toxic culture, employees are paralyzed in making decisions due to micro-managing of the manager who can hide behind formalized rules and regulations. Managers who are not effective will rely on rules to make decisions instead of allowing their subordinates to have the autonomy to make their own decisions. As a result, an action which could be resolved immediately moves through a slow-winding bureaucracy because the subordinates are not allowed to make a decision which would solve the problem.

Furthermore, toxic managers believe that it is easier to make no decisions instead of making any decisions. This lack of action can foster unethical behavior if the subordinates believe that the manager does not care about the "means" and instead just focuses on the end result. In addition, employees could be less likely to correct unethical decisions if they do not have the authority to make those adjustments.

Remote work is not considered "real" work

The coronavirus pandemic has certainly proved the belief that remote work is not considered to be "real" work incorrect, although traditionally any work done outside the workplace setting was not given the same degree of validity as work done "at the office." The underlying premise for this belief goes back to Douglas McGregor's Theory X framework. Under a Theory X belief system, employees are considered to be lazy and will not be fully productive unless they are constantly monitored and watched by the manager. As a result, it is assumed that remote-based employees are taking "advantage" of their situation by not being as productive as they could be. An alternative non-toxic view of employee behavior is McGregor's Theory Y in which the manager can trust the employee to be as productive as possible without constant monitoring. This approach is based on the belief that as long as the manager hires the employees who are the most qualified and have the best skill set to succeed in their job, the manager can delegate responsibilities to the employees and, thus, does not have to monitor their actions.

Entrepreneurship is not encouraged

A toxic manager with a toxic workplace culture does not encourage nor expect employees to be driven by innovation and creativity. From a narcissistic perspective, toxic managers want all the credit for any ideas that are generated from the business unit. Therefore, any employees who are entrepreneurial driven are not wanted, since these employees and their ideas are a direct threat to the power base of the manager. Therefore, entrepreneurial-driven employees will quickly leave the toxic environment and move to another firm so that their ideas can be encouraged and rewarded by the new firm.

An "us versus them" toxic workplace climate

Toxic managers view themselves at a different level and, therefore, a different standard than their subordinates. In a potentially hypocritical behavior, toxic managers will follow the "do as I say, not as I do" philosophy. During the coronavirus pandemic, inconsistencies were evident in how top-level managers and other employees of the firm were treated. While rank-and-file employees would be furloughed or terminated, top-level executives of the same firms were hesitant to willingly either reduce or eliminate their own compensation to represent their commitment to the other employees and to the firm. Other perks such as traveling first class, having large expense accounts, and having expensive company cars create both a tangible and intangible separation between management and the other employees. This separation and alienation can be seen in how employees communicate with each other. If there is a "wall" between management and employees, employees are more likely to comment that "management" needs to look at this issue rather than a more appropriate "we" need to look at this issue.

Preferential treatment

A common and highly unethical action is for the manager to give unwarranted preferential treatment. Unwarranted treatment is a necessary condition because giving rewards for superior preference can be perceived as preferential but justified treatment. For example, the top sales representative in the department may be rewarded with being given the top potential future clients of the firm. While other sales representatives may perceive that this is unfair and preferential, in reality the top performer receives a reward of future sales based on the sales representative's previous performance. However, if a sales representative is given the best new leads not due to his/her performance but instead were given them because both the sales representative and the manager graduated from the same university, this is an example of unethical preferential treatment.

Therefore, if there is not a justification for preferential treatment, this unethical behavior can further create a toxic workplace environment. If the treatment is unwarranted, then envy and jealousy will be created by those employees who do not receive the preferred treatment by the manager. In addition, it may further reduce the incentive for the employees to be productive if the signal sent by the manager is that employees are rewarded not based on merit but on favoritism by the manager.

Darwinist approach to employee performance

In a toxic culture, under-performance results in potentially public humiliation where the manager can treat the employees with cruelty and no sense of empathy. By using the first stage of Kohlberg's stages of moral development, managers shame low performers through verbal abuse and/or the downgrading of the employee's job requirements. Embracing Machiavelli's advice that it is better to be feared than loved, toxic managers treat low performers in a way that these actions will be a signal that any employee who does not perform in an adequate manner will be treated in the same manner.

One fundamental flaw with this approach is that the low performance may be based on the employee's skill set not matching the requirements of the job. Since decisions had already been made to hire and train the employee, the manager must realize that the weakness of the employee's performance could be based on not having a proper fit with the job. Therefore, an alternative and more effective approach may be taken in firms that have a more supportive work environment. In highly employee supportive firms, under-performing employees are not ridiculed, but instead are helped, coached, and given feedback. The employee may need additional training to get up to speed with the specific skills needed for the job. The employee is also re-evaluated to determine whether there is another job which more closely matches their skill set. This re-adjustment by the firm results in the employee becoming fiercely loyal to the firm since the employee was given a second chance to thrive in the workplace.

Managers forcing employees to write fake reviews

As narcissists, toxic managers believe that they are effective, valuable assets for the firm. As a result, they believe that other employees will also see these valuable traits. However, Glass Door and other websites allows former employees to air their differences in the public arena. Toxic managers obviously do not want this information to become public since it would deter excellent potential employees from applying for jobs with the firm. One method to counteract these negative disclosures is to demand that the employees write positive reviews on job recruiting websites to counterbalance the actual negative reviews.

Ethical values are not applied

While a firm may have credos, mission statements, and comprehensive codes of ethics, these documents have no value if the employees do not embrace the values associated with these beliefs. For example, one of the most corrupted firms in the history of commerce, Enron, had a Code of Ethics which was 63 pages in length. In a positive work environment, ethical values are automatically incorporated in the decision-making process, which makes concerns about the application of ethical values a moot point. In a toxic work environment, ethical values are ignored and the message from the manager and the firm is that only results matter and not the process to get those results.

Bibliography

Denning, Tim. 2019. A Toxic Work Culture Is Forcing High-Performing People to Quit. *LinkedIn*. June 25.

Dvorak, Phred and Megumi Fujikawa. 2018. Medical School's Exam-Rigging Against Women Prompts Furor in Japan. *The Wall Street Journal*. August 7.

Kohlberg, Lawrence. 1981. *The Philosophy of Moral Development*. New York: Harper & Row.

Milgram, Stanley. 1963. Behavior Study of Obedience. *Journal of Abnormal and Social Psychology*. 76:4. 371–378.

Scheiber, Noam. 2015. Fake Cover Letters Expose Discrimination Against Disabled. *The New York Times*. November 2.

Stanwick, Peter A. and Sarah D. Stanwick. 2016. *Understanding Business Ethics*. Third Edition. Thousand Oaks, CA: Sage Publications.

Van Bavel, Jay J. and Tessa V. West. 2017. Seven Steps to Reduce Bias in Hiring. *The Wall Street Journal*. February 20.

Zarkadi, Theodora and Simone Schnall. 2012. "Black and White" Thinking: Visual Contrast Polarizes Moral Judgment. *Journal of Experimental Social Psychology*. 49: 355–359.

6 Ethics and environmental sustainability

Essential summary

Mahatma Gandhi observed that the "Earth provides enough to satisfy every man's need, but not every man's greed." This simple sentence explains the complexity of the ethical issues related to the natural environment. As with any decision a manager makes, there are always tradeoffs in how the decision impacts others. However, decisions related to the natural environment, by their very nature, have global implications. This chapter focuses on the potentially complex conflict of a firm relative to its financial and environmental performance. While a firm must identify and serve the needs of all its stakeholders, one of its most important stakeholders, the natural environment, does not have an explicit voice in the discussion of environmentally based decisions.

The chapter starts by discussing environmental sustainability. Just as managers need to be good stewards of the firm's finances for long-term sustainability, this belief is also true for being good stewards of the firm's natural resources. The next section addresses the tragedy of the commons, which has been discussed by humans since the time of Aristotle. The tragedy of the commons highlights that resources will be exploited if there are no control mechanisms in place.

The chapter continues with a discussion of who should take responsibility and the subsequent burden of environmental-based decisions made by the firm. Through the lens of environmental justice and Not In My Backyard (NIMBY), this section of the chapter highlights that people globally do not share an equal burden when decisions which have a negative impact on local communities are implemented.

The chapter concludes with an in-depth discussion of one of the most important concepts related to the sustainability of life on earth, climate change, and global warming. The continuing rise in global temperatures will make solutions to climate change only more critical in the future. This last section on climate change links back to the first section of the chapter on environmental sustainability. Without climate change solutions, there will no longer be sustainability for the natural environment and for the living organisms who reside on this planet.

Ethics and environmental sustainability

Since there are a finite level of resources in the world, environmental sustainability is based on the belief that each generation must be good stewards of the resources they control. A simple way to view sustainability is ensuring that future generations have the same access and enjoyment of the world's resources as the current generation. It is from this framework that managers must incorporate how to use resources of the firm based on the understanding of how those decisions not only impact the current needs of the stakeholders, but also consider their future needs. An easy exercise to reinforce the importance of environmental sustainability is for the decision maker to reflect on whether his or her children would be satisfied with the decisions made today related to the use of natural resources.

It is not only managers of firms that must incorporate environmental sustainability in their decision-making process. It is the responsibility of all stakeholders, whether it is individuals, firms, governments, or local communities, to understand how their decisions impact each other as stakeholders. The United States Environmental Protection Agency (EPA) defines environmental sustainability as the acknowledgment that everything that is required for long-term sustainability of humanity and the earth is either directly or indirectly related to the natural environment.

Examples of highly sustainable companies

Since 2005, the Canadian research firm Corporate Knights has ranked highly sustainable firms globally with revenues of over $1 billion based on metrics related to sustainability. In its 2020 ranking, the top three firms were Orsted, Chr. Hansen Holding, and Neste Oyj.

Orsted

Orsted is a Danish-based renewable electricity provider that has transformed its business by moving away from fossil fuels. As the largest electricity company in Denmark, Orsted moved away from using coal and shifted to offshore wind energy to power its electricity facilities. By 2020, it reduced its carbon emissions by 86 percent since the transformation started and its goal is to be coal free by 2023 and be carbon neutral by 2025. By 2040, Orsted wants to expand its carbon-neutral footprint to include its supply chain and energy trading. Orsted has developed 20 sustainability programs in its shift to a carbon-neutral firm. Orsted's offshore wind farms generate energy to over 13 million people with its goal of reaching 50 million people by 2030. Orsted is the first electricity firm to be ranked number 1 in the Corporate Knights ranking. The company had moved up from being ranked 70 in 2019.

Chr. Hansen Holding

Chr. Hansen Holding is a Danish bioscience firm that develops natural microbial solutions for the food, beverage, nutritional, pharmaceutical, and agricultural industries. The focus of the firm is to preserve foods such as yogurt and milk, protect crops using natural bacteria instead of pesticides, and develop alternatives to antibiotics for animals. By focusing on "good bacteria" Chr. Hansen Holding can preserve foods longer to increase safety and reduce food waste. Good bacteria which is created by Chr. Hansen Holding is incorporated into crop strains and the seeds are harvested and available to farmers. The crops which include the bacteria in its molecular structure become naturally protected against disease and pests, and the plant roots are also protected. Chr. Hansen also uses its natural bacteria in the development of probiotic solutions as an alternative to using antibiotics to battle bacteria in animals and humans.

Neste Oyj

Neste Oyj is a Finnish petroleum refinery and marketing company with revenues of over 15 billion euros in 2020. In the past, Neste refined oil to be burned which generated greenhouse gas emissions. Neste is shifting away from refining fossil fuels. By 2019, more than 50 percent of Neste Oyj investments were not in fossil fuel-based refining but were instead focused on renewable biofuels. Twenty-five percent of Neste's revenue comes from biofuel refining and the biofuel division generates 50 percent of the firm's profits. Neste's customers are represented in a diverse selection of industries including transportation, aviation, polymers, and chemicals. Neste is the largest producer of renewable diesel and renewable jet fuel which is refined from waste and residues. Neste's renewable diesel has reduced greenhouse gas emissions by 90 percent compared with fossil fuels. By 2022, Neste is projected to produce over 1 million tons of renewable jet fuel annually, which has an 80 percent smaller carbon footprint compared to fossil jet fuel. Neste is also developing a process to convert waste plastics into a raw material which can be used to produce new plastic. Neste's goal is to reduce the level of greenhouse gas emissions by at least 20 million tons annually by 2030.

The tragedy of the commons

The tragedy of the commons is based on the primal nature of humans. Based on the philosophy of Aristotle and later revived by Garrett Hardin, the tragedy of the commons is based on the belief that free access and unrestricted use of any finite resource will ultimately result in the resource being ruined through overexploitation. From a natural environment perspective, the tragedy of the commons will predict that the eventual consumption of all-natural resources and the ineffective disposal of certain resources will occur globally due to the lack of uniform control over its use.

Hardin presents the argument that there is a finite amount of natural resources on earth, and that humans need to be good stewards to these natural resources. Being good stewards would result in the conservation of natural resources and the efficient disposal of waste instead of the overconsumption of these resources. Hardin gives the example of cows grazing on open land. If there are no restrictions nor cost for the cows to graze on the land, there is an incentive for the farmers to bring as many cows as possible onto the land since it is considered to be a "free good."

However, the more cows that each farmer brings to the land, the less grazing opportunities for other farmers with their cattle. Therefore, the existing farmers with their cattle would receive all the financial benefits of the open land. The farmers who were not given the opportunity to have their cattle graze the land would receive all the negative financial impacts of the commons.

The commons are not only grazing land but other natural resources such as air, water, soil, forests, and energy resources. Therefore, if there is no accountability of the actions of a person using the commons, there will always be a motivation and temptation to exploit the natural resources that are considered to be commons.

The tragedy of the oceans

The world's oceans are an example of a miraculous ecosystem. While designed to be both a sustainable and bountiful source of food, the tragedy of the commons has had a significant impact on the ability of the oceans to thrive in the future. By their very nature, the oceans are one of the greatest commons that humans have had access to for thousands of years. But, without proper controls, the oceans are impacted by pollution and overfishing. Since boats and ships can dump tons of material into the oceans without reprimands, the oceans have become an underwater landfill.

Plastics play an especially dangerous role in marine life survival since fish and other marine creatures can swallow and get caught in the plastic. It is estimated that 8 million tons of plastic make their way into waterways and eventually are deposited into oceans. In 2015, it was estimated that China was responsible for 27.7% of the world's mismanaged plastic waste ending up in oceans. A distant second place was Indonesia with 10.1 percent, while the United States only had 0.9 percent of the world's mismanaged plastic waste.

Countries around the world have been negatively impacted by overfishing. Again, the tragedy of the commons dictates that every fisherman would catch as many fish as possible if there were no restricted quotas on the catch amount. It is estimated that 90 percent of fisheries globally are either fully exploited or overexploited in their fishing areas. Some experts have estimated that from 1970 to 2019, the number of fish in global oceans has dropped by 50 percent. In addition to the ocean being a commons, there are many countries in East Asia that give fisherman financial subsidies to catch fish, motivating the fisherman even more to overfish when it is possible.

The natural environment as a stakeholder

The natural environment can be a stakeholder because it has a vested interest in the operations of every firm globally. While the natural environment does not have a physical voice, its interests are presented through proxy representation of NGO environmental groups. The true impact of the stakeholder status of the natural environment is represented in the acknowledgment of firms that the "needs" and "expectations" of the natural environment should be incorporated into the decision-making process of the managers of the firm.

The argument against identifying the natural environment as a stakeholder is based on the philosophical belief that only humans should be considered in the evaluation of ethical issues. Under this definition, a non-human entity such as the natural environment would not be considered in the consequences of an individual's actions since the natural environment did not have an opportunity to present its concerns related to the actions of the individuals. Both the philosophical arguments presented by utilitarianism and Kant are based on the belief that nonhuman entities should not be factored into the decision-making process.

As a counter argument, a holistic stakeholder perspective would argue that an all-encompassing and more realistic perspective would refer to utilitarianism as providing the greatest good to the greatest number of living things, not just focusing exclusively on the greatest good to humans. Furthermore, Kant's view on focusing on the duties of individuals can be expanded to recognize the individual's duty to all living things and not just the impact the decisions will have on other human beings.

Environmental justice

Environmental justice can be defined as the right of individuals and local communities to be protected from the implementation of decisions that have been made by firms or governments which have a negative environmental impact on stakeholders. The protection of this justice is based on the belief that every individual should have the right to live in a local community which is both clean and healthy. The "injustice" of these decisions is based on individuals suffering the negative impact of environmental actions who were not involved in the creation of the environmental burden these decisions generated in the first place.

Traditionally, environmental injustice is based on a disproportionate number of communities with specific demographic characteristics including nationality, race, ethnicity, or social-economic class receiving the burden of negative consequences of environmentally based decisions. There are three reasons why lower economic-based areas are more vulnerable to bear the burden of environmental injustice: siting, move-in, and vulnerability.

Siting occurs when neighborhoods with lower income levels are selected for negative environmental impacts such as landfills and waste storage facilities since the people in these neighborhoods have been traditionally disenfranchised and, therefore, do not have a voice to protest the decision of the location of the new facility which has a negative environmental impact.

Move-in occurs when people with lower income levels move and live in areas where the price of housing is lower due to environmentally based facilities near the local community. It is these lower property prices that become part of the justification for the firm locating a facility in a certain area which has a negative environmental impact. By being able to acquire land at a cheaper rate, the firm can argue that the validity of the decision was based on trying to minimize the financial impact to the firm. Therefore, a vicious circle is created based on lower property prices attracting facilities which have a negative environmental impact, leading to even lower property prices.

Vulnerability occurs when people living in lower-income neighborhoods do not have the same access to healthcare and other health-related amenities, including clean water and fresh food. As a result, people living in these neighborhoods are more vulnerable to having health-related issues based on the release of pollution and/or toxins from the environmental facilities.

Environmental racism in Houston, Texas

In a Houston neighborhood of 2,000 residents, the people are surrounded by refineries, chemical plants, sewage treatment facilities, and hazardous waste sites. The Harrisburg/Manchester neighborhood in Houston is 96.7 percent Hispanic with many of those families living below the poverty line. This is a common example of environmental injustice, which has recently been relabeled by some NGOs as environmental racism.

This neighborhood must deal with the release of toxins from nearly 30 refineries and chemical plants located close to their houses. In close proximity to the neighborhood there are 21 Toxic Release Inventory (TRI) reporting facilities, 11 facilities that generate hazardous waste, 4 facilities that treat, store, or dispose of hazardous waste, 9 facilities that discharge a large amount of air pollutants, and 8 major stormwater discharging facilities. It is estimated that 90 percent of the people in the neighborhood live within 1 mile of a chemical facility. On average, 484,000 pounds of toxic chemicals are released into the neighborhood annually from the 21 TRI facilities. The cancer rate in Harrisburg/Manchester is 22 percent higher compared with the overall Houston area.

The elementary school in the neighborhood had to be relocated when it was discovered that the children were accumulating a high level of concentration of lead in their bodies. The school was relocated to a site which is 30 feet away from the two busiest highways in Houston. The result was that the children traded lead exposure for higher levels of carbon monoxide (CO), nitrogen oxide (NOx), sulfur oxide (Sox), and other volatile organic compounds (VOCs) from vehicle emissions. Environmental injustice can occur in local regions within a country or this injustice can be exported to other less economically developed countries. One example of this international transfer of environmental injustice is the shipping of electronic waste to African countries.

The case of environmental injustice and toxic eggs in Ghana

Electrical and electronic equipment which no longer functions becomes electronic or e-waste. E-waste can be generated from personal computers, printers, televisions, mobile phones, refrigerators, and air-conditioning units. Within this e-waste there can be numerous toxins including mercury and lead, as well as precious metals such as gold, copper, nickel, and cobalt.

Therefore, there is a two-edged sword related to the desirability of obtaining e-waste. E-waste is shipped to less economically developed countries due to the demand for capturing the precious materials in the e-waste. Once the e-waste reaches these countries, it may not be managed properly to ensure that the toxins do not impact local neighborhoods. As was mentioned in the previous section, environmental injustice is based on individuals being negatively impacted by environmental issues which the individual did not create. The United Nations established the Basel Convention, whose goals are to: support environmentally sound management; prevent the illegal transfer of e-waste to developing countries such as Ghana, Tanzania, and Nigeria; and support the development of building capacity globally to better manage e-waste.

An example of the deadly result of environmental injustice related to e-waste occurred in Ghana. The e-waste was illegally shipped from Europe and was sent to the Agbogbloshie slum located in the capital of Ghana, Acca. The e-waste was dumped into a landfill area so the local residents could have access to the electronic components. The residents would open up the waste products and search for the precious metals. When these electronic products were opened, they would release dangerous toxins and polychlorinated biphenyls (PCBs) and other harmful materials. These toxins would seep into the ground and would be found in the soil and then ultimately in the plants and grass that grew in the soil.

An analysis conducted on free-range chickens that ate the forage near the e-waste landfill found that a single egg laid by the chickens had over 220 times the legal limit of chlorinated dioxins, based on the standards established by the European Food Safety Authority. The soil of the surrounding area is saturated with dangerous toxins yet the individuals collecting the e-waste do not wear any protective gear. The slum is home to an estimated 80,000 people whose survival is based primarily on capturing precious metals and copper wire from e-waste.

Sam Adu-Kumi of the Ghana Environmental Protection Agency stated that:

> Europe needs to contend with its toxic e-waste, rather than routing it to developing countries, such as Ghana where hazardous chemicals contaminate populations (especially the vulnerable) and the environment, as a result of mishandling and existing indiscriminate disposal practices... African countries should not be used as an e-waste dumping ground any more, as we do not have the technological capacity to deal with waste containing high levels of persistent organic pollutants.

Not In My Backyard (NIMBY)

A counterbalance to the environmental injustice movement is the Not In My Backyard (NIMBY) philosophy. NIMBY is based on the belief that local communities can organize and block the proposed development which has a negative environmental impact on the community. In the past, a primary focus of the NIMBY movement was to block the building of waste treatment facilities and landfills near impacted communities. The negative impact of these investments can include health risks, financial risks, and quality of life risks.

NIMBY versus wind power

As an alternative energy source to fossil fuels, wind power has been perceived as a long-term viable alternative option which does not generate greenhouse gases (GHG) emissions. Countries within the European Union have agreed to shift certain percentages of their energy generation to renewable energy sources. Wind power seems to be the optimal alternative energy source since it produces energy without emitting any emissions into the atmosphere. However, many local communities do not want to embrace wind energy.

The wind turbines block views for the local residents and the turbines can be seen for a mile on a clear day. In addition, the shadow caused by the turbines creates what is termed a "shadow flicker" which can frighten animals and the turbine's noise can be loud enough so that the residents can hear it constantly. Other concerns of local residents include the building of infrastructure and power transmission lines to transfer the power. The loss of scenic views can also have a negative impact on local tourism. The gigantic blades of the turbines can also kill flying species such as birds and bats. The turbines not only produce noise but also create continuous vibrations which can be felt by the local residents. Despite the closeness of the turbines, there are relatively few, if any, financial benefits to the local community.

Germany versus wind power

With the development of the Energiewende initiative, the German government has embraced energy transformation through the adoption of alternative energy sources. Germany has been driven to use alternative energy sources since it established long-term environmental goals, including that 65 percent of Germany's energy consumption would come from nonnuclear renewable energy sources by 2030. In 2019, 42 percent of Germany's energy came from nonnuclear renewables. Germany also set the goal of no longer using coal to generate energy by 2038. However, the growth in wind turbines has slowed significantly in Germany. While Germany had 29,456 turbines in 2019, that was just a net increase of 243 turbines from 2018.

The wind turbine industry had to start addressing difficult challenges in 2017 after the German government stopped granting financial subsidies to wind farm projects. The other significant challenge was the rise of local communities protesting building wind farms in their area. While nationally, Germans overwhelmingly support wind power, that support was not present in communities which would be impacted by the introduction of a wind farm. This is an excellent example of NIMBY. People nationally can greatly support environmental initiatives if they are not located near their communities.

In 2020, it was estimated that there were over 900 local protest movements in Germany trying to stop the expansion of the government's wind farm program. The protest groups highlighted their concerns including danger to wildlife, adverse health effects for the local residents, and the devaluing of their property. Many of the protests used local courts to try and block the wind farm developments, generating costly delays for the developers in the hope that the developers would give up on projects. In 2019, the development of 325 wind turbines were challenged in the courts with 60 percent of the cases based on legal challenges by environmental groups. Issues such as environmental injustice and NIMBY can be complex and potentially difficult to resolve. However, the driving force for the use of alternative energy sources is to try to reduce the impact of climate change globally.

Ethics and climate change

Greenhouse gases (GHG) have warmed the earth for millions of years and are a necessary source of warmth for the survival of living things on earth. The creation of GHG can be both natural such as methane generated by cattle or man-made such as the burning of fossil fuels. The burning of wood is also a source of GHG that can be natural, such as forest fires started by lighting, or man-made. It is estimated that a few days of the energy emitted by the sun is equivalent to all the energy stored within fossil fuels. This powerful source of energy is also necessary for the long-term survival of all living things. It is estimated that 70 percent of the energy from the sun is absorbed by earth and the other 30 percent of the energy directed at the earth is reflected back into space.

The origins of climate change started with the rise of GHG during the Industrial Revolution. This increased concentration of GHG started to thicken as layers around the earth's atmosphere. As the level of GHG increased, some of the 30 percent of the energy that was going back into space was redirected back to earth. This phenomenon was due to some energy not breaking though the GHG layer around the earth. This phenomenon is similar to a greenhouse. In a greenhouse, the sun shines into the structure and the physical structure traps some of the heat from the sun and it remains in the greenhouse to facilitate the growth of plants. The greenhouse effect results in the earth becoming hotter over time as more energy from the sun is captured and redirected back to earth.

This effect started to occur in the late 1800s when the Industrial Revolution warranted the use of fossil fuels to generate energy for manufacturing plants. In the over 200 years since the Industrial Revolution, GHG emissions have increased significantly due to the burning of fossil fuels and, to a lesser extent, deforestation.

The global impacts of climate change

There are several current negative impacts of climate change around the world: increased temperatures, rising sea levels, natural disasters, political and security risks, human health risks, and the impact on wildlife and ecosystems.

Increased temperatures

Increased temperatures impact the ability of humans to function in regions which are most significantly impacted by climate change. The ability to live, work, and eat can be permanently altered due to climate change. Heatwaves can result in heatstroke and other health conditions which can be fatal. The ability to move from one location to another can be severely limited due to extreme heat conditions. The ability to grow crops and maintain livestock is also threatened due to increasing temperatures. High temperatures can also result in crops either being less productive or dying out due to the changing climate conditions.

Rising temperatures can also alter the composition of the crops, resulting in the reduction of the nutritional content in grains and cereals. It is estimated that by 2050, 150 million people will have a protein deficiency due to climate change and 1.4 billion will not have the necessary iron in their diets. Furthermore, it is estimated that 600 million people could be impacted by the decline in the nutritional value of rice due to climate change.

Rising sea levels

One of the most dramatic impacts of climate change is rising sea levels. As the earth's temperature increases, glaciers globally melt with the subsequent water deposited in the oceans. The net result is that an estimated two-thirds of the world's largest cities will be threatened in the future since these cities are located in coastal areas which are low lying and, therefore, prone to flooding. The dramatic significance of this flooding is that it becomes permanent. The land that was previously above sea level could permanently be submerged below water level due to climate change. Millions of acres will be lost forever as the rising sea levels permanently alter the configuration of the earth's land mass.

It is estimated that if the sea levels rise by 2 meters or 6.60 feet by 2100, between 470 and 760 million people will no longer have a place to live since the land where they live will be submerged. Among the major cities which would be submerged by this sea level rise would be major portions of London and Shanghai. In the United States, this higher sea level would result in estimated damage to coastal property of between $238 billion and $507 billion, with New York, Miami, and Boston being significantly impacted.

Natural disasters

Rising temperatures result in the atmosphere holding more water vapor, which results in higher rainfall and runoff when the air is saturated and much drier conditions when the air is not saturated. This will result in a shift of weather patterns where some areas will experience extreme droughts while other areas will receive more intense and sustained rainfall. The net result is that it is predicted that certain regions of the world will endure extreme droughts, floods, and storms.

Political and security risks

Climate change can create political instability due to factors such as food shortages. If a country's food and water yield has been reduced due to rising temperatures, the citizens of the country will demand that they receive access to food and water for survival. If the government fails to fulfill this request, political unrest can develop and could create rebellion and riots.

Extreme drought can create permanent shifts in the migration patterns of the citizens within the country, which also shifts the political representation of the citizens. The underlying challenge for governments is that since rising temperatures will continue to increase, so will the potential political instability.

Human health risks

The emissions from the burning of fossil fuels can create significant health problems. The World Health Organization has estimated that approximately 7 million people die globally due to the result of pollution caused by fossil fuels. Health issues related to fossil fuels include not only premature mortality, but also workdays lost and other health-related issues. Other health issues related to climate change include increased rates of malnutrition, malaria, diarrhea, and heart disease. Rising temperatures also increase the breeding capabilities of certain insects, which results in increases in waterborne diseases as well as health issues related to insect bites.

Wildlife and ecosystems

Rising temperatures have changed the habitat conditions and migration patterns of wildlife. Wildlife will move northward toward cooler temperatures, which disrupts the natural ecosystem. The food for the wildlife may not move, or not at the same rate as what is desirable for the wildlife. Food such as flora and insects are also impacted by rising temperatures, which threatens the long-term survival of numerous species.

This threat of eventual extinction includes not only land species but also ocean-based creatures. Rising temperatures in the oceans impact coral reefs and plankton and other living materials which are paramount to the long-term survival of fish and other marine species. The ocean temperature has risen by 0.74 degrees C (1.3 degrees F) over the past 100 years, which has resulted in oceans becoming more acidic, impacting marine animals' reproductive systems and long-term survival along with the slowly dying coral reefs.

Climate change and Bangladesh

In an extreme example of environmental injustice, the country of Bangladesh will receive a disproportionately negative impact due to rising temperatures of the earth. Bangladesh's topology makes it extremely vulnerable to any increase in sea level. Most of the population is located near the ocean and the land is near sea level, which results in a devastating impact on the nation. Due to its land level near sea level, very minor increases in the sea level will result in catastrophic damage due to permanent flooding of low-lying areas. These areas will be swallowed by the ocean, never to be seen above water again. Some experts predict that sea levels could rise by 3 feet by 2100, which would result in the coastal cities of Bangladesh being completely underwater.

Bangladesh will be impacted in two different but related impacts of climate change. The sea levels will rise as glaciers globally melt and the sea level will rise in the Bay of Bengal where Bangladesh is located due to the melting glaciers from the Himalayan mountains. Therefore, Bangladesh will have locally higher sea levels than other parts of the world due to glaciers melting globally as well as locally. The melting glaciers of the Himalayan mountains is a two-edged sword for Bangladesh since this is a major source of clean water. Therefore, once the glaciers have completely melted, the overall sea levels may subside near Bangladesh, but the country will lose its primary source of clean water.

Another problem is that as the sea water moves inland, even if it does not stay permanently inland, the salt from the sea water will make the soil ungrowable. This would have a devastating impact on the local farmers. The impact of soil salinity will result in local farmers not being able to plant as many crops, resulting in a decrease in supply, which will result in increased food prices for the people of Bangladesh. On average, Bangladeshi families spend between 30 and 40 percent of their total household expenditures on rice. If the price of rice increases significantly, these families would no longer be able to afford to buy this primary food staple.

While Bangladesh only generates 0.4 metric tons per capita of carbon emissions, climate change will fundamentally change the configuration of the country. In comparison, the United States generates 17 metric tons per capita of carbon emissions and the United Kingdom produces 7.1 metric tons. Therefore, Bangladesh's low carbon emission rate but catastrophic impact of climate change demonstrates how environmental injustice is not just local in nature.

Bibliography

Basel Convention: Controlling Transboundary Movements of Hazardous Wastes and Their Disposal. www.basel.int/Implementation/Ewaste/Overview/tabid/4063/Default.aspx

Beaumont, Peter. 2019. Rotten Eggs: E-Waste from Europe Poisons Ghana's Food Chain. *The Guardian.* April 24.

Bender, Ruth. 2020 Germany's Push for Wind Power Encounters Resistance. *The Wall Street Journal.* March 10.

Char Henson.com. www.chr-hansen.com/en

Crawford, Julianne. 2018. Environmental Racism in Houston's Harrisburg/Manchester Neighborhood. *Stanford Earth: School of Earth, Energy & Environmental Sciences.* March 15.

Harding, Garrett. 1968. The Tragedy of the Commons. *Science.* 162:2859: 1243–1248.

Henderson, Rebecca M., Sophus A. Reinert and Mariana Oseguera. 2020. Climate Change in 2020: Implications for Business. *Harvard School Publishing.* January 8.

Neste.com 2020. *Corporate Profile.* www.neste.com/corporate-info/who-we-are/business

Orsted.com. 2020. *The Most Sustainable Company in the World.* https://orsted.com/en/sustainability/our-stories/worlds-most-sustainable-company-2020

Smith, Noah. 2019. The World's Oceans Need a Bailout. *Bloomberg.* October 31.

Stanwick, Peter A. and Sarah D. Stanwick. 2016. *Understanding Business Ethics.* Third Edition. Thousand Oaks, CA: Sage Publications.

Stanwick, Peter A. and Sarah D. Stanwick. 2020. *International Management: A Stakeholder Approach.* Northampton, MA: Edward Elgar.

Strauss, Karsten. 2019. The Most Sustainable Companies in 2019. *Forbes.* January 22.

Todd, Samantha. 2020. Who Are the 100 Most Sustainable Companies of 2020? *Forbes.* January 21.

7 Ethical issues in the developing world

Essential summary

As the world population moves closer to 8 billion people, individuals and firms must understand the importance and viability of the needs and expectations of people throughout the world. This chapter focuses on issues related to countries which have developing or emerging economies and starts with a discussion on how entrepreneurs who focus on social issues can yield both financial and social rewards for their actions.

The chapter continues with a discussion of the people who are located at the bottom of the economic pyramid. Those in extreme poverty or close to extreme poverty have specific challenges which are not being properly served by firms who have a global presence. This lost opportunity highlights the traditional bias by managers who perceive that people in emerging economies are "high risk" and, therefore, should not be a focus of their strategic visions.

One method to alleviate extreme poverty is the introduction of microfinancing, which gives potential entrepreneurs the opportunity to establish their own business through microloans which do not require any collateral. Another opportunity to improve the standard of living for farmers in emerging economies is to offer the farmers a fair trade premium for their product, which helps ensure the long-term sustainability of their farms.

The chapter concludes with a discussion on global human rights. While in many countries, people take these human rights for granted, this is not the case in every country. Numerous categories of human rights violations globally attack the core belief that everyone should have the protections and rights of being a human being.

Social entrepreneurship

Social entrepreneurship is based on the creation of an organization whose business model focuses on basic global human needs that are not currently being served. Social entrepreneurs embrace the concept that a firm can be profitable while addressing a social cause. It is this dual drive of profitability and social responsibility that motivates social entrepreneurs to succeed in both of these dimensions. In the development of a long-term self-sustaining model, social entrepreneurs are able to succeed financially, which allows them to pursue a sustainable social mission.

Four types of capital for social entrepreneurs

To effectively achieve their goals of financial and social success, social entrepreneurs must be able to develop and exploit to their advantage four types of capital: financial capital, social capital, environmental capital, and aesthetic capital.

Financial capital

Financial capital is based on the creation and growth of financial capital within the firm. Financial capital is a critical component needed by any entrepreneur. It is imperative for social entrepreneurs to obtain and maintain a steady flow of financial capital in order to guarantee the long-term financial sustainability of the firm, which results in the long-term sustainability of the firm's social mission.

Social capital

Social capital is based on "wealth" that is created for local communities and society as a whole by fulfilling the social mission of the firm. This social capital not only serves the unmet needs of current individuals, but it also sets the foundation of establishing long-term relationships and expansion of the social network of the firm.

Environmental capital

Environmental capital is based on "wealth" that is created by the firm being good stewards of its natural resources. The firm's environmental capital can be used by the firm to differentiate itself in the marketplace from its competitors. Furthermore, being proactive in relation to environmental issues is something that is consistent with and expected from social entrepreneurial firms.

Aesthetic capital

Aesthetic capital is based on the intangible "wealth" that is created by employees within the firm by giving them the intrinsic value of feeling good by helping others. While it could be argued that financial capital is the most critical form of capital, it could also be argued that aesthetic capital is the most valuable capital for a social entrepreneurial firm. It is the aesthetic capital that motives all the employees of the firm to maximize their effort. It is the aesthetic capital which gives the firm the opportunity to recruit and select highly qualified potential employees without necessarily having to offer the same compensation levels as other firms.

The aesthetic capital can become the "secret sauce" for the social entrepreneurial firm since the employees are unified in their tasks of ensuring that the firm achieves its financial and social goals. This secret sauce also translates into a good story. By pitching the story to a venture capital firm or a corporate sponsor, the aesthetic capital emotionally links the social entrepreneur's vision with financial funding. Therefore, for those social entrepreneurs who have created a non-profit organization, transference of the story to the sponsors is paramount in the long-term sustainability of the organization. It is the synchronization of the vision and values of the organization and the individual and corporate sponsors that will define the long-term financial sustainability of the organization.

However, the firm should not take its aesthetic capital for granted. The employees have the same values and commitment as the founder and managers of the firm. Therefore, these employees need to be heard. Management must give the employees opportunities to present ideas and suggestions as the firm navigates its strategic position. Part of the "feel-good" factor of the employees is an acknowledgment that their ideas matter and that their creativity is a significant intangible asset for the firm.

Sanjit Bunker Roy: A true social entrepreneur

> First they ignore you, then they laugh at you, then they fight you, then you win.
>
> (Mahatma Gandhi)

In 1972, Sanjit Bunker Roy established Barefoot College in a village in the Rajasthan State of India. However, Barefoot College is not a traditional college. The curriculum is based on training women from different parts of the world as solar engineers. The women, who have not had opportunities for a formal education, and in most cases are illiterate, are taught how to install, maintain, and operate household solar-powered lighting systems. As an Indian educator, Roy provided these women the opportunity to become highly skilled technicians. Due to the initial high rate of illiteracy, the women are taught in sign language and color codes to master the knowledge and be able to go back to their villages to help generate electricity from the solar-powered systems.

In India, where 70 percent of the population live in rural areas, 40 percent of which do not have access to electricity, Roy believed that his program would have a significant impact on the lives of thousands of Indian people. Without electricity, rural people are at higher health risk due to having to use kerosene for lighting and firewood for cooking. In addition, the lack of electricity impedes economic development in the local villages, which results in migration to India's cities.

When the operations started in India, Roy also established a non-traditional approach to select the students attending Barefoot College. The typical student is an illiterate grandmother. Roy stated that "Young people are untrainable... They are obsessed with training certificates, which we do not provide, and once they get the training, they leave the village looking for money and opportunity in the city." Older rural women, on the other hand, are more likely to stay in the village with their technical skills. While the new students may seem bewildered at first, Roy used a demystified and decentralized approach in teaching the students. By 2011, there was a staff of 400 who teach approximately 50 women per session. The teachers are alumnae of the school. Roy expanded his operations to seek entrepreneurial-minded women in different parts of Africa.

Traditionally in India and parts of Africa, rural women have little power and self-confidence. This program not only reverses those attributes, but the graduated students are a valuable resource in their communities. The community pays graduated students a salary as solar engineers because the community recognizes the value of the skills the engineers provide to the village. The women receive a wage and the village receives electricity for the first time.

From 2006 to 2011, it was estimated that over 500 babies in Ethiopia were safely delivered in solar-lit homes instead of using kerosene or candlelight. In Malawi, the benefits of solar-lit homes include eradicating rats and scorpions in houses, which results in safer home environments. In Sierra Leone, solar-electrified equipment allows for the refrigeration of immunization products.

Barefoot College is now in over 70 countries and has regional facilities in Africa, Latin America, and Southern Asia. In Latin America, it is operating in 17 countries and the first 70 solar engineers from the Latin American program were able to bring electricity to over 11,000 people. In Africa, Barefoot College has operations in Burkina Faso, Liberia, Senegal, Zanzibar, and Madagascar.

The skills now acquired by the women include the ability to install integrated circuit boards for solar home lights and off-grid solar units, which can generate up to 500 kilowatts of electricity daily. The women are also taught to be able to assemble solar lanterns, compact fluorescent lamps, parabolic solar cookers, and solar water heaters

Barefoot College funding model

As was mentioned in the previous section, a social entrepreneurial enterprise cannot survive without financial capital. Barefoot College takes a customized approach to match funding with its social initiative. Barefoot identifies an area of need from its list of Least Developed Countries. It then identifies potential donors whose objectives closely match the objectives of that social initiative. Barefoot also seeks out firms whose corporate social responsibility initiatives match the newly identified project in both the program's mandates and goals.

Therefore, the full circular model starts with the identification of the country and region in which Barefoot College wants to develop a new initiative. The second step is to identify funding partners whose vision agrees with the new program. The third step is to identify indigenous NGOs who would be willing to support the project. The fourth step is the identification of key individual donors who also embrace the new program. The fifth step is the execution of the new program and the circle starts again for the new project.

For example, the Starbucks Foundation formed a partnership with Barefoot College to focus on promoting women's economic leadership and wellness in tea communities for seasonal workers in India. The program empowers the women with personal development skills and technical training on the solar devices. The program also teaches the women about self-care, nutrition, and sanitation with the goal of positively impacting over 3,000 local community members. Other corporate partners include Goldman Sachs, Apple, Philips Lighting, Oracle, United Way, Bank of America, Rio Tinto, Sierra Club, Conde Nast, and World Wildlife Fund (WWF).

The bottom of the pyramid

The bottom of the pyramid refers to the part of the global population that earns, on average, the equivalent of $1,500 or less annually. In 2002, an estimated 4 billion people were included in this bottom rung of the pyramid. The next rung up the pyramid represents individuals making between $1,500 and $20,000, and was was calculated to include between

1.5 and 1.7 billion people. The top rung of the pyramid is those individuals making more than $20,000 annually, which encompasses between 75 and 100 million people.

The people at the bottom of the pyramid have traditionally been ignored by most global firms since they are perceived to be "high risk" and "low resource" customers. Since these markets are not considered by global firms, billions of people are either not served or underserved by firms which could benefit by having these markets included in their overall global growth strategy.

Investments in these emerging economies will serve the needs of numerous stakeholders of the firm by having a positive impact on the customers and local communities, the country itself through increased tax revenue, and the firm's investors through increased levels of profitability. In addition, investments in the firm can lead to lower levels of poverty through the development and expansion of physical and financial markets as well as financial institutions.

Strategies for the bottom of the pyramid could not only increase the financial performance of the firm but the firm could recruit locally based emerging entrepreneurs with the experience of understanding the needs and expectations of potential customers within the country. One of the challenges for the global firms entering these markets is the adjustments that need to be made with product lines.

Due to the potential customers' limited financial resources, the firm needs to ensure that they offer the customers products that are in small unit sizes, have low profit margins, and have high potential volume in order to make this foreign investment sustainable in the long term. The ability to sell products with a low profit margin is directly related to the ability of the firm to have an extremely efficient cost structure so they can "afford" to sell the products at a lower price point.

When C.K. Prahalad wrote about the bottom of the pyramid in the early 2000s, the outlook of serving these markets may have been considered overambitious and unrealistic. However, 20 years later, the outlook looks much more promising and attainable. Despite the common thread that targeting these markets was too risky and that it is the responsibility of governments and NGOs to provide the services needed to serve these people, global firms have started to embrace the growth potential of serving the bottom of the pyramid.

The data shows that the economic pyramid has shifted over time. While 4 billion people in 2002 earned less than $1,500 (USD), by 2017 the bottom of the pyramid has been reconfigured to include annual incomes of less than $10,000 and includes 3.5 billion people. By 2017, 1.1 billion people earned between $10,000 and $99,999 annually, 391 million earned between $100,000 and $1 million, and 36 million earned over $1million. From 1990 to 2019, the World Bank estimated that 1.1 billion people had earned enough money annually to move out of extreme poverty, which is defined as earning less than $1.90 daily. An estimated 40 people per minute had overcome poverty in 2019.

There has been a significant reduction in extreme poverty globally, which has opened up numerous entrepreneurial opportunities to identify and address social issues globally and has resulted in the shrinking of the gap between the bottom and other levels in the economic pyramid. One of the major advancements available to all people globally is technology and the use of cell phones. The ability to communicate in an inexpensive way has allowed the expansion of growth opportunities in both learning and commerce. The current technology adopted globally allows, for example, the electronic transfer of money, which makes physically going to a bank branch obsolete. This is especially important in rural areas globally where there is not a physical presence of a financial institution.

The emerging economies located at the bottom of the pyramid have been identified by the International Monetary Fund as having some of the fastest-growing economies globally. The strategy for global firms to capture these markets are based on five components: companies with a higher purpose; trust and community before transactions; lower-cost design; hybrid products of luxury and economy; and social codes and norms.

Companies with a higher purpose

Firms understand that they need to serve the needs of all stakeholders. While pressure to perform well financially is always a paramount objective, firms need to acknowledge and embrace the needs and expectations of stakeholders from a holistic perspective. Customers, employees, and local communities want to understand the overall vision of the firm, which includes the firm's commitment to social responsibility. Therefore, if the firm expands its operations to emerging markets and effectively serves the needs of those markets, the firm has an opportunity to demonstrate its social commitment through its actions.

Trust and community before transactions

As with any market, the firm must realize that the building of trust between the firm and the customer is critical for both short-term and long-term success. Global firms cannot just "drop" the product into a new market and expect it to sell just because it sells in other countries.

The customers need to be educated about the product and local sales-people are needed to present the attributes of the product and provide answers to the questions posed by the customers. It is imperative that global firms focus on customer service in not only the selling of the product but also in the aftersales service to customers. The creation of a trusted relationship not only helps future sales but gives the firm valuable feedback as to what changes are necessary as the customers needs and tastes evolve over time.

Lower-cost design

Global firms can use business analytics to determine not only patterns of buying behavior but also facilitate the ability to develop products and provide services at lower price points. By identifying what attributes are the most desirable to the customers, the firms can reconfigure the design of existing products to meet the unserved needs of the emerging economies. The reconfiguration not only includes the use of cheaper materials, but it can also aid in the firm's ability to completely redesign the product to be able to sell it at a lower price point.

Hybrid products of luxury and economy

Every customer wants to buy a product or use the service from the perspective that this purchase is good value for the customer. Good value means that the perceived value of the product is higher than the purchasing price of the product. As a result, the global firm can use its knowledge and expertise to develop multiple lines of products that serve the needs of all of its global customers. In addition, products that are developed to target the bottom of the pyramid may have a market in other countries. Furthermore, based on the price point, products that were targeted from one rung of the pyramid may be desirable to customers in other rungs.

Social codes and norms

Global firms have the ability to have a positive impact on the social codes and norms of local communities at the bottom of the pyramid. Each individual's daily life is based on transactions to obtain food, water, shelter, and other basic necessities. Firms can help build a social infrastructure to make these transactions easier. For example, in Kenya, there are numerous roads that do not have identification markers such as names and numbers.

This results in a chaotic attempt to provide services such as mail delivery. The Kenyan-based company MPost developed an app which allows the use of the customer's mobile number as a postal address.

The impact of COVID-19 at the bottom of the pyramid

The news that extreme poverty had decreased over the past 20 years is now tempered with the impact of COVID-19. The World Bank predicts that this pandemic will have a disproportional impact on the global poor due to job losses, the loss of payment for services, rising prices for goods, and the disruption in services related to education and health care.

It is expected that poverty rates will increase globally as the world economies attempt to recover from a deep recession which could actually become a depression in some countries. The pandemic will eliminate almost all of the progress made from 2015–2020 related to global poverty. The World Bank estimates that between 40 and 60 million people will slide down to the lowest rung of the economic pyramid, which is extreme poverty of less than $1.90 daily. It is estimated that the global extreme poverty rate will increase to approximately 9 percent in 2020. For those earning less than $3.20 daily, the projected increase will affect between 40 million and 150 million people globally and for those earning less than $5.50 daily, the estimated growth will affect between 70 million and 180 million people.

Microfinance and the bottom of the pyramid

One of the great success stories to come from targeting people at the bottom of the pyramid is the development of the microfinance system by Muhammad Yunus. Yunus, an economics professor, would discuss economic theory in the classroom and yet would observe an economic system which failed the people of Bangladesh who were battling poverty.

Yunus established the Grameen Bank, whose function was to set up microloans for poor villagers in Bangladesh. Yunus realized that the villagers were potential entrepreneurs who never had a chance to be able to start their own businesses due to lack of funding. In a classic example of Catch 22, traditional financial institutions demand collateral value in return for lending money. This requirement ensures that the bank can seize the asset put up for collateral if the individual defaults on their loan. This is a vicious cycle since the individual does not have any collateral to use to back the loan because the individual has no money. Yunus saw that this cycle cannot be broken through traditional lending practices. The villagers who did have access to money had to pay extremely high interest rates to the money lenders because of the "high risk" of the lenders' investment.

Therefore, Yunus set up his own lending operation and initially loaned out a total of $27 to 42 villagers and did not ask for collateral. Instead, Yunus trusted that the receivers of the loans would pay back Yunus as expected. The entrepreneurs did pay back the loan. Yunus proved that people with limited resources can be trusted and that those people take accountability and responsibility for their actions. Due to his initial success, Yunus created the Grameen Bank, which has millions of borrowers and provides billions of dollars of loans. When Grameen Bank started, 97 percent of the borrowers were women. The high percentage of women was due to their intense motivation to be entrepreneurs to use their profits to help their children and families improve their standard of living.

Microfinancing gives the opportunity for potential entrepreneurs to financially flourish to not only the benefit of the entrepreneur, but also to the local village by providing critical products and services. An additional benefit of microfinancing for the local villagers is that the entrepreneurs learn knowledge and skills which also will be beneficial to the local community.

A typical example of a microfinance investment would be for a woman to borrow $50 from a microfinance institution (MFI) to buy chickens. The woman sells the eggs to the villagers, who now receive a fresh source of protein. The woman uses the money from the selling of the eggs to pay back the loan. The MFI has a close relationship with the woman and gives her advice on how she can grow her business. The MFI wins because the loan money is returned to them and the entrepreneur wins because she now has a sustainable business. The MFI then "recycles" the $50 loan money to another entrepreneur.

Fair trade

The simple philosophy behind fair trade is that farmers in emerging countries need to obtain enough money from their crops to be sustainable in the future. Fair trade programs ensure that the farmers are able to receive the equivalent of a living wage and are able to survive as farmers. The fair trade system was created to adapt the free market-based trade system to properly serve the needs of the farmers. In some markets globally, the commodity pricing of produce and other food products does not generate enough income for the farmer to be sustainable. Part of this sustainability is the ability for the farmers to afford to buy seeds for the next season's harvests of produce.

Fairtrade International is the global organization which certifies those participants that want to be involved in the fair trade system. Fairtrade International works with over 1.66 million farmers and workers in 738 countries. From 2014 to 2020, fair trade producers and farmers received over 500 million euros in money that was a premium to the free market price of their produce. Fairtrade certification not only results in the farmers receiving more money, but it also ensures the working conditions meet the standards defined by Fairtrade International. Fairtrade certifications can occur for bananas, cocoa, coffee, cotton, flowers, gold, sugar, tea, wine, and other products. The Fairtrade International certification process focuses on three areas: economic standards, environmental standards, and social standards.

Economic standards

The economic standards of the certification process are to ensure that the farmers have a safety net against falling prices, which allows long-term planning. Fairtrade also builds and strengthens long-term partnerships, which requires the buyers to provide pre-financing to the farmers if requested.

Environmental standards

The environmental criteria for Fairtrade certification include that the farmers have ecologically and agriculturally sound practices, which include responsible water and waste management. The farmers are also expected to preserve the biodiversity and soil fertility of their lands through minimal use of pesticides and agrochemicals. Fairtrade certification does not allow the farmers to use hazardous materials and forbids the selling of any genetically modified organisms (GMOs).

Social standards

The social criteria for Fairtrade certification require a work environment with non-discriminatory employment practices, pay rates to the workers at or above the minimum wage rate, and employees must have the right of freedom of association and collective bargaining. The employer must have safeguards pertaining to worker safety and health. Forced labor and child labor are forbidden.

Cocoa and fair trade

It is estimated that 90 percent of the world's cocoa is grown on small family farms by approximately 6 million farmers. The cocoa bean, which is used to make chocolate, grows in a very precise climate. The climate must be hot, rainy, and tropical, and the farmers must protect the beans from wind, sun, pests, and disease. A typical cocoa tree can start to reach maximum yield levels after five years and can be productive for another ten years.

Between 2016 and 2017, the price of cocoa decreased by over one-third and some cocoa trees had become unproductive due to disease and age. The sustainability of the cocoa industry became even more threatened by the number of failing family farms.

Through the Fairtrade certification process, farmers in Cote d'Ivoire and Ghana were able to develop a sustainable model through the payment of the Fairtrade Premium price. In 2017, cocoa farmers had received over 38 million euros in Fairtrade Premium of which a portion was used for investments in agricultural tools and farming supplies. Companies which make or sell fair trade chocolate include Aldi, Ben & Jerry's, ASDA, Nestle, Marks & Spencer, Mars, Oxfam, Sainsbury's, and Starbucks.

Human rights

Human rights can be defined as the universal rights of all individuals. Human rights are a cornerstone of the existence of human life on earth. Regardless of the decisions made by firms and governments, all stakeholders should have protected human rights.

In December 1948, the United Nations' General Assembly adopted the Universal Declaration of Human Rights. The Declaration is grouped into seven major categories: personal rights; legal rights; civil liberties; subsistence rights; economic rights; social and cultural rights; and political rights.

Personal rights

An individual's personal rights include: the right to life, the right to claim a nationality, the right to be formally recognized before the law: the right to be protected against cruel and inhumane treatment and the legal protection against being discriminated based on the individual's race, ethnicity, sexual orientation, and religious affiliation.

Legal rights

An individual's legal rights include having access to a process which can resolve basic rights violations; the presumption of innocence until proven guilty in any legal matter; the legal guarantee to be tried in a fair and impartial manner; the legal protection against being charged with retro-active laws; the legal protection against arbitrary arrest and detention; and protection against arbitrary interference with a person's family, home, or reputation.

Civil liberties

An individual's civil liberties include the rights of having freedom of thought, conscience, and religion; the freedom of being able to express one's own opinion; the freedom of movement and residence; and the freedom of peaceful assembly and association.

Subsistence rights

An individual's subsistence rights include the ability of the individual to obtain food and be able to establish a standard of living which provides the individual and his/her family with health and well-being.

Economic rights

An individual's economic rights include the ability to work, rest, have leisure activities, and have social security.

Social and cultural rights

An individual's social and cultural rights include the ability to access education and the ability to be able to participate in cultural events within the local community.

Political rights

An individual has the political rights be able to participate in government and be able to participate in elections which are transparent and legitimate.

Five steps to ensure the protection of human rights

There are five steps that firms are required to follow to ensure that employees and other stakeholders have their human rights protected. The first step is for the firm to develop and implement a global comprehensive human rights policy which is supported by the top-level managers of the firm. The second step is to ensure that the human rights policy has actionable policies and guidelines which every employee is aware of and agrees to abide by in the firm's operations. The third step is to ensure that the human rights vision and beliefs of the firm are incorporated into the strategic and operational decision-making process. The fourth step is for the firm to develop a formalized training program so that employees understand their roles in ensuring the human rights of the firm's stakeholders are protected. The fifth step is to establish and maintain a formalized monitoring system to ensure that the firm's employees follow its human rights policies. One NGO which monitors human rights actions globally is Amnesty International.

Amnesty International

Founded by Peter Benenson in 1961, the original focus of Amnesty International was to attempt to obtain amnesty for prisoners of conscience. These prisoners of conscience were arrested because of their beliefs, the color of their skin, their ethnic background, or their religious beliefs. Amnesty International became a major force in identifying human rights injustices and received the Nobel Peace Prize in 1977. Over an extended period of time, the focus and mission of Amnesty International evolved to include not only prisoners of conscience but also other types of global social injustices. Amnesty International now focuses not only on human rights violations, but also on the protection of refuges and migrants and seeks the global abolishment of the death penalty, torture, the use of deadly police force, and gun violence, together with protection regarding gender, sexuality, and identity issues. Amnesty International also focuses on issues related to climate change, corporate accountability, disappearances of activists, freedom of expression, social injustice for indigenous people, and the ability of people to live with dignity.

Amnesty International has over 7 million people working on the causes related to social injustice and is funded solely through private donations. Amnesty International has a presence in over 70 countries and has developed a "panic button" app which activists can push in order to inform Amnesty International that the individual has been arrested or detained.

Bibliography

Amnesty International website. www.amnesty.org/en/

Barefoot College website. www.Barefootcollege.org

Fairtrade International website. www.fairtrade.net/

Lankarani, Nazanin. 2011. Generating the Unlikeliest of Heroes. *The New York Times.* April 18.

Prahalad, Coimbatore K. 2004. *The Fortune at the Bottom of the Pyramid: Eradicating Poverty Through Profits.* Upper Saddle River, NJ: Wharton School Publishing.

Prahalad, Deepa. 2019. The New Fortune at the Bottom of the Pyramid. *Strategy+Business.* Spring: 94. January 2.

Stanwick, Peter A. and Sarah D. Stanwick. 2016. *Understanding Business Ethics.* Third Edition. Thousand Oaks, CA: Sage Publications.

Stanwick, Peter A. and Sarah D. Stanwick. 2020. *International Management: A Stakeholder Approach.* Northampton, MA: Edward Elgar.

World Bank website. www.worldbank.org/en/topic/poverty/overview

Index

Printed in the United States
by Baker & Taylor Publisher Services